First Official Cabinet photo—The Oval Office—1981

(left to right)
Back row: Raymond Donovan, Donald T. Regan, David A. Stockman, Drew Lewis, Samuel R. Pierce Jr., James Watt, Edwin Meese III, Malcolm Baldrige, Richard Schweiker, William J. Casey.
Middle row: Terrel Bell, William French Smith, Jeane Kirkpatrick, James Edwards, William Brock, John R. Block.
Front row: Alexander M. Haig Jr., Ronald Reagan, George Bush, Caspar Weinberger.

The Thirteenth Man

Books by Terrel H. Bell

Effective Teaching: How to Recognize and Reward Competence

A Philosophy of Education for the Space Age

Your Child's Intellect: A Guide to Home-Based Preschool Education

A Performance Accountability System for School Administrators

Active Parent Concern

Fiction

The Prodigal Pedagogue

The Thirteenth Man

A Reagan Cabinet Memoir

|||||||||||||||||||||||||||||||||||||||||||||||||||||||||||||||||||||||||||||||||||||||||||||||||||||||||||||||||||||||||||||||||||||||||||||

TERREL H. BELL

former United States Secretary of Education

THE FREE PRESS
A Division of Macmillan, Inc.
NEW YORK

Collier Macmillan Publishers
LONDON

*The Free Press
A Division of Macmillan, Inc.
866 Third Avenue, New York, N.Y. 10022*

Collier Macmillan Canada, Inc.

Printed in the United States of America

*printing number
1   2   3   4   5   6   7   8   9   10*

Library of Congress Cataloging-in-Publication Data

Bell, Terrel Howard
  The thirteenth man.

  Includes index.
  1. Bell, Terrel Howard   . 2. Cabinet
officers—United States—Biography.   3. United States—
Politics and government—1981–   4. Education and
state—United States—History—20th century. I. Title.
E840.8.B45A3   1988   353.84′4′0924   87–25992
ISBN 0–02–902351–3

To those stalwart Bells who made
three U-Haul treks to Washington:
     Betty Ruth
     Mark
     Warren
     Glenn
     and Peter

Contents

Prologue

As I cruised down Lee Highway in my official Lincoln Continental en route from my Arlington home to Capitol Hill in Washington, I had an animated conversation with my new chauffeur, Charles Holton. As the newest, and in seniority of my department, the most junior member of President Ronald Reagan's cabinet, I couldn't see why it was really necessary to have a telephone in the car that had been provided me by the federal government.

I was on my way in to the House Chamber in the Capitol, and looking forward to playing a small part in an historic event when I asked him about it. "I don't understand why the White House communications people make such a big fuss over telephones, Charles," I said. "There won't be anything so urgent in my work as secretary of education that it requires instant access to a phone while I ride to and from work."

"Well, Mister Secretary, I've driven for several cabinet members down through the years. You need to remember, if I may say so, that you gotta be reached at all times—day and night."

"But, Charles, I'm hooked up to the White House switchboard by direct line in my office. I'm also wired into them from home. Would you believe there are White House phones on all three levels of my town house in Arlington?"

"In all my driving experience, the cabinet members have had busy phones in their cars," Charles said.

"I'm not new to Washington, Charles," I assured him. "I was here before—in a lesser position—as U.S. commissioner of education under President Nixon and President Ford."

"But you're cabinet now, Mister Secretary. That makes all the difference. You gotta be reached when the president says to get Secretary

Bell. Then, maybe, the secretary of state, the attorney general, or the secretary of defense might need to talk to you.''

''I don't think there will be many times when Ronald Reagan will be calling me,'' I replied with a touch of irony.

''But even if you're not in your car,'' Charles added, in his effort to justify an expensive mobile telephone system, ''if you're some other place in a meeting, I have to be waiting outside to take any calls and then come in and get you. That's happened a lot of times, Mister Secretary. Just you wait and see!''

My first stop was a reception hosted by the *Wall Street Journal* in honor of the new president's cabinet. I had a special, personal reason for being there with the other cabinet members. The *Journal* had published an editorial that morning praising the president's acumen in selecting a very distinguished cabinet. The only exception was his final choice. The article went on to explain what a terrible decision it had been to pick me as secretary of education. I had less than warm thoughts about those soon to greet me in their reception line, but I was not going to show that I had a sore tail over the matter by being the only cabinet member not to show up at their event.

My plan was to arrive a bit on the late side. I would pay my respects to my critics and leave for the House Chamber for the really big event of the evening, the State of the Union message. It would be Ronald Reagan's first major address to the nation since his inauguration just a few days ago. I was looking forward to that as much as I was dreading the reception. As it turned out, the reception was okay and the State of the Union event became a small disaster for me.

A president's appearance before a joint session of the House of Representatives and the Senate is a major occasion. Scheduled to be present in the huge House Chamber that evening, in addition to the lawmakers and the cabinet, were the U.S. Supreme Court and ambassadors from foreign countries.

The television networks bring the message to most of the nation. It is a very impressive gathering, history in the making, and I was looking forward to sitting up front with the rest of the cabinet. I was still a bit starry-eyed at being in such a high office.

I was born in a small town in Idaho and grew up in poverty. At times, despite years of government service, I still felt overwhelmed by all that was happening to me. It was both exciting and humbling to be working side by side with so many of the nation's chief decision makers. The State of the Union address was to be preceded by the entry of the new cabinet into the House Chamber. To be among these celebrities was heady stuff.

As we drove from the reception to the Capitol, Charles Holton had an opportunity to demonstrate the uses of instant telephone access at all times. When the phone rang, Charles answered calmly, then told me over his shoulder that it was an urgent call from Jim Baker, the president's chief of staff.

"I am glad I reached you, Ted," Jim explained. "I hope you don't mind my calling so late. You see, I'm just learning all the details of my job. I just found out a few minutes ago that it is unlawful for all those who, by law, are in line of succession to become president to be gathered together at the same place at the same time. As you know, seniority is determined according to the date the cabinet department was created. There are thirteen departments and you rank thirteenth. In view of that, would you mind going home and watching the State of the Union address on television? I know the president will appreciate it, and I am sorry that I was so late catching you."

I responded as graciously as I could. I assured Jim Baker that I would be pleased to see that we did not violate the law. He hung up and I asked Charles Holton to turn around and take me back home to Arlington.

As I walked in the door, Betty was tuning in the TV set so she could get a glimpse of her husband marching down the aisle with the cabinet. She looked very surprised.

"What are you doing here?" she exclaimed.

"I got sent home," I responded, hearing the dejection in my voice. "But don't worry," I added brightly. "Before this is over I might be president of the United States!"

Despite my temporary gloom, I thought the event amusing at the time, a mere technicality to be taken in good humor. In retrospect, it was really something of an omen. In this administration the Department of Education and its concerns were indeed to be last—and thirteen is not a notoriously lucky number.

CHAPTER 1

Return of a Potomac Recidivist

When I left Washington for the second time, in the fall of 1976, I had no expectation of ever returning. In early 1981 the attraction, of course, was the opportunity to serve as a member of Ronald Reagan's cabinet, but given the nature of my proposed new role, there were ample reasons not to take it on. Reagan had promised the voters that he would abolish the Department of Education. I had not only favored it, but I had testified before a Senate committee in support of Jimmy Carter's bill to establish the department. Tax cuts and budget cuts were in the offing. So, why accept the Reagan invitation to join his cabinet as U.S. secretary of education?

I wanted the job! I was even arrogant enough to think I could teach Ronald Reagan to use his considerable persuasive powers to fight for the nation's schools and colleges. I felt all I needed was a chance to get on the inside, where I could preach the gospel of education to the movers and shakers of the new administration.

Moreover, at the get-acquainted stage before I was formally offered the job, I was not convinced that a cabinet-level department was essential to American education. But I did know that we needed federal-level leadership and that we needed an education agency that was not a captive of HEW or some other major department whose primary function was something distant from education. My HEW tenure had made that clear to me.

During my years in Washington under the Nixon and Ford administrations, as deputy commissioner and then the twenty-first U.S. commissioner of education, my boss, the secretary of HEW, was Caspar Weinberger. He was a splendid man to work for. He was bright, not nearly so conservative as many think, and had a sharp, aggressive mind and a great sense of humor. I suspected that in those days after the November 1980 elections, when Ronald Reagan was selecting his cabinet, Cap Weinberger put in a few good words for me. He was a Reagan in-house man. If anything, I was in the outhouse so far as Reagan might be concerned. I had never met him. I knew no one else on the Reagan team. It had to be Cap who was responsible for initiating my candidacy for the cabinet post.

I persisted in this belief even after meeting Ed Meese, counselor to the president from 1981 to 1985, in a San Diego restaurant booth on January 2, 1981. Meese had boasted in Washington that the Department of Education was a "great bureaucratic joke." He had promised the early demise of the cabinet agency over which I would have jurisdiction. What is more, he promised to persuade the new President to "cut to the bone" and eventually eliminate all federal financial assistance to education.

In defending the role of research and the gathering of data to add some wisdom to education decision making, at that meeting, I reminded Ed Meese and his companion, Martin Anderson, director of the Office of Policy Development, that the research arm of the department, the National Institute of Education, had been created on the initiative and with the strong support of Richard Nixon. It was not a creation of the Jimmy Carter regime.

"I always knew they impeached Nixon for the wrong reason," was Anderson's smiling response. I glanced over to see Ed Meese nodding his head in vigorous agreement with Anderson's remark.

Pennington James, the president's headhunter, who was also present, described to me the great distinction that would be mine if I could, some day early in the Reagan administration, walk into the Oval Office and hand the president the keys to the Department of Education and say: "Well, we've shut the abominable thing down. Here's one useless government agency out of the way."

What I heard from Ed Meese was especially unnerving, and I knew from our first meeting that he'd be a challenge. It became readily apparent to me that he placed too much emphasis on the private sector. He held public schools and universities in disdain. If the president-elect shared his views, I would have at the least a very lively time in Washington.

During this meeting in San Diego I grew fascinated with Ed Meese and his cocksure certainty in all matters, which was displayed both in what he said and how he said it. Here was a man who literally detested the federal government. He viewed the upcoming Reagan presidency as a magnificent opportunity to smash the government programs that had created a "welfare state."

As I was to discover, Meese was destined to be the champion of the far right in the White House. He was in touch, I found out later, with those who hoped for a true rightist social and economic revolution. Such ultraconservatives as Howard Phillips, Paul Wyrich, and Richard Vigurie would soon be beating a path to Meese's door in the west wing of the White House.

That first personal contact with the Reagan regime came after Penn James had talked to me on the telephone several times. This started rumors flying in Salt Lake City, where I was then serving as the commissioner and chief executive officer of the Utah System of Higher Education. After the third call from Penn, it became apparent to others in my office that I was under consideration for a position with the Reagan administration. But most of the conversation centered on my views of other possible candidates. All the cabinet had been announced except for the secretary of education. There was even speculation that the president-elect would not fill the post at all—just leave it vacant until it was abolished.

I had arrived at our agreed meeting place in San Diego grouchy, tired, and irritated at myself for even making the trip. The Salt Lake airport was fogged in with January weather. I had had to take a 2 A.M. Amtrak train to Las Vegas and then fly on to San Diego.

We were to meet at the Admirals' Club of American Airlines, but neither Meese nor Penn James had made any arrangements, so we couldn't get in. This situation was not what one might expect in an interview organized by two of the highest-level emissaries of a newly elected president of the United States. We finally sat down in a restaurant booth where, in the next hour or so, I learned about Ed Meese's right-wing views, with special emphasis on education. There was no spectacular meeting of the minds, to put it mildly, and my mood and demeanor did not improve as I listened and replied. When I returned to Salt Lake City I was convinced that the new Reagan administration was not for me. I assumed that the president-elect's views were reflected in what I had heard at the San Diego airport. I could not reconcile myself to this. During my return trip to Salt Lake City, I did not entertain any further consideration of becoming a member of the new Reagan cabinet. The interview just finished had taken care of that. I shifted my concern to preparing for the opening session of the Utah Legislature. That was the job at hand.

Then came a series of surprises. The first and the biggest surprise was a call four days later to meet Ronald Reagan at Blair House in Washington. Newspaper speculation concerning the president-elect's final cabinet selection had suddenly stopped including my name. I knew from past Washington experience that names are floated and leaked to the press in a series of trial balloons as a technique designed to draw out any significant opposition. The president-elect could thereby avoid the embarrassment of announcing my or any name as his choice and subsequently having to withdraw it in a clumsy retreat in the face of opposition.

I checked in at the Mayflower Hotel and prepared to meet Ronald Reagan for the first time. I reviewed papers and press accounts of issues in the campaign prior to the November 1980 election. I wanted to refresh my mind on what Reagan had said about education issues.

When I arrived at Blair House a crowd of newspaper reporters and TV camera crews was gathered at the front door. As I hopped out of a cab, this group swarmed in my direction. I ducked and ran up to the main entrance into Blair House. I was ushered to an upstairs sitting room, where I waited to meet the President-elect. Ed Meese came by to chat for a moment, but he never referred to our recent meeting in San Diego. It was all small talk until Ronald Reagan appeared.

Meese introduced me. Reagan sat down on the couch across from me. He seemed relaxed, willing to talk and get acquainted, and obviously eager that I feel at ease.

Since I was seeing him for the first time, I recall that I looked him over thoroughly. He was tanned and healthy, although he had more wrinkles than I had noted on television and in his photographs in newspapers and magazines. He was immaculately dressed; his clothes fitted his personality and his build. His dark brown hair glistened, and every hair was in place. From his gleaming eyes it was obvious that he wore contact lenses.

His handshake was firm. The veins on the back of his hands stood up with the bluish tinge that is typical of elderly people. There was an abundance of brown age spots on the back of his hands. He wore cuff links; his shoes shone as he leaned back and crossed his legs comfortably.

The president-elect was warmly attentive. I found myself very comfortable in my first conversation with him. I knew that his quest for this last member of his cabinet had been delayed because of lack of conviction concerning its importance. But he displayed interest in and concentration on what I had to say. He explained his concern about a cabinet-level Department of Education. He emphasized his interest in schools and colleges and his firm conviction that education should be primarily a state rather than a federal responsibility. He expressed fear of federal control of education.

The most surprising and encouraging thing to me was the fact that Ronald Reagan showed none of the scorn or bitterness toward federal financial assistance programs that I had heard from Meese when I expressed my concern that the new Reagan administration not be too hasty to abandon financial aid to college students and federal financial assistance to improve learning opportunities for disadvantaged and handicapped elementary and secondary school students. I was cheered by this, for I had anticipated views more like those I had heard in San Diego. The president didn't sound like an enemy of the schools. I was even more encouraged by what he did not say, because I knew he was choosing his education chief and this was his chance to warn me about what must be done.

It was easy for me to affirm my interest in strengthening both local and state responsibility for education; I believed in this. Mr. Reagan said his chief concern was the question of federal control. He wanted to act soon to change the structure of the Department of Education. When I reminded the president-elect that I had testified in support of the bill to create the department, he asked if I could support an alternative. I said I was willing to consider establishing an independent federal agency of lesser status than a cabinet department, but I also explained my opposition to placing education back in HEW.

I then told the president-elect that if I were selected to be his secretary of education I would want the responsibility for supervising the staff work that drafted alternatives to the department structure. The president-elect answered, "Well, okay, let's go for it!" And with that casual response I became a member of the president's cabinet.

As I arrived back at the Mayflower Hotel I carried with me both elation and the burden of the reality that Ronald Reagan had selected me as his secretary of education. I called my wife in Salt Lake City to break the news.

"Can you believe it?!" I exclaimed, blurting out quickly what had just happened at Blair House.

"I knew it!" Betty groaned. "This will be the third time we drag just about everything we own across the continent to Washington. But I hope this time it won't be in a U-Haul truck."

"The same rule applies as when I was appointed U.S. commissioner of education," I replied. "If you take a post that is presidentially appointed, you move at your own expense. But this time I'll dig up the money to move you first class."

"No way! Not if it comes out of our pockets," said Betty. "We can't afford that."

"But how do *you* feel about it?" I asked.

"I guess we can handle it," Betty said. "If you want the job, it's okay with me. You'll just have to give me time."

"But time is what we don't have. This is the eighth of January and the President is sworn in in twelve days from now. I know you'll be expected to be here with the other cabinet wives."

"The Senate won't even vote to approve your appointment by then," Betty said. With two previous stints in Washington she was wise to the ways of Congress.

"It won't matter. We'll still be expected to participate in all the ceremonies and events that go with the installation of a new administration."

"We can work it out," was Betty's final word.

I put the phone down and flopped on the bed to think of all that had happened in the past two hours. I had so much to do in a very short time. I still held the responsibility of my Utah posts. The chairman of the Board of Regents, Don Holbrook, knew of my interview with Ronald Reagan, but my termination would be abrupt and difficult for the regents, who had supported and worked with me for the past four years.

The president-elect's staff had told me he would announce my appointment tomorrow at 2 P.M. After that, I must make my phone calls and be ready to answer questions from the press. I thought of associates in Utah higher education and friends and relatives whom I should contact. This led me to my immediate family—to my brothers and sisters who would want to hear the news.

And that brought me back a flood of memories of my mother, Alta Martin Bell, a widow who had raised nine children with no money. I was third from the bottom in that group of Bell kids. My father was killed in an accident in 1929 when I was eight years old. My mother was left penniless at the beginning of the Great Depression of the 1930s. It was her encouragement and constantly upbeat attitude that had pushed me on my way. I could not share the news with her. She had died in 1962. But her buoyant spirit and teachings were very much alive. My mother was a master at encouragement. She talked about a world full of opportunities and what I could do to realize my potential. We had talked endlessly about what I should do when I left Lava Hot Springs to go to college, and there had never been any doubt that I would go. She had poured that expectation over my growing mind for years. The discussion was about what I would do, not whether it was possible to do it.

She had no knowable reason to be so positive and optimistic. We lived in poverty—in a small, four-room house with no indoor plumbing. Growing up in a family of ten in a tiny house with only two bedrooms might be called an experience of togetherness. With so little money, life was harsh. We scraped and scratched for every dime. We kept a huge garden that extended out to the vacant lots on both sides of our scraggly, unpainted wood-frame house. My mother made the best home she could for all of us. The house was old; the cupboards were literally bare; and the old outhouse was distant, dark, and smelly. Mother was broke; the Great Depression promised no work or prospects for any of us. But she felt she was rich because she had "nine million-dollar kids." And I was one of them, and I had to perform accordingly.

How I wished I could call her just to tell her that the new President of the United States had decided to appoint me to his cabinet! She would have been thrilled with the news, but knowing her, not entirely surprised.

My early years in Lava Hot Springs taught me to appreciate simple things like being warm when it was cold outside. It was best to get to bed early in our cold, cold January rooms. The one sleeping in the middle was warmed by a brother on each side. You covered up all the way including your head, leaving just a breathing hole in the heavy blue denim quilt. (We made quilts out of the remains of blue denim clothing.) In the morning the frost around the breathing hole attested to the temperature outside and in.

It also signified the enriched or impoverished condition of the wood-pile. An all-night fire was possible only when there was ample fuel. I learned to be an expert with an ax. Our fuel warmed us twice. You were fairly well warmed up with the exercise of chopping dried aspen logs, then the fire in the heating stove and the kitchen stove warmed you a second time. We watched the wood supply for the long run and the short. There had to be an ample pile of logs for the winter. This was hauled in from the mountains during the summer months. A large pile of dried aspen logs was essential to our winter survival. The supply in the wood box had to be replenished daily to keep our mother warm while we were off at school. This required chopping each day in lengths that would fit our two stoves.

Soon after my father's death a cow was added to our family's meager assets. She came to us out of the cultural traditions of our religious affiliation. I was raised in the Mormon church. The admonitions to be independent and self-sufficient were key commandments in my growing years. To receive charity from others without doing work in return for what was received was contrary to the basic tenets of our faith. Mormons help you to help yourself, and they do not want you to be denied the blessing the Lord will bestow on you as a consequence of hard work.

This fundamental tenet led to my receiving an unusual gift from the local Mormon bishop, J. R. Maughan. He gave me a cow! It was a shrewd act on his part. Since the cow was mine, the responsibility for her care, feeding, and milking was fixed upon me. For several years this animal provided a source of vital nutrition for a widow and her children. Her milk gave me rock-hard teeth that I have kept to this day. It also gave me a tough and wiry muscle and bone structure. If I stretch I can reach a height of five feet five inches. But that was genes, not poverty-induced malnutrition.

We worked on farms in the summer to earn enough hay to feed the cow in the winter. She was a mean old beast. As a young boy I learned to love and hate her. She had to be milked twice a day. Rain or shine, clear weather or bitter cold winter blizzard, that beast had to be milked and fed. In the dark of night after a full day at school I was out on a wooden milk stool hand-pumping the milk from a warm and smelly cow's udder.

She could kick, sidestep, twitch, and turn. The best time for her to switch her tail across my face was immediately after she had had a wet bowel movement that coated her tail. She always had to urinate at least four times during each milking. These were timed to catch me off guard, and her aim at the milk bucket was uncanny.

This ill-tempered critter needed a firm hand. I learned to respond to her antics with stern retribution. A string of difficult milkings led to her being tied very tightly to a cedar post so there was no slack for her to move her stubborn head. Good behavior was reinforced, and bad behavior was punished. Through the years she and I never learned to trust each other, but we developed a cold-war stance of alternating skirmishes and peaceful coexistence.

But if my daily and nightly wrestling with the cow were a torment, school in Lava Hot Springs was a joy. My life in Lava Hot Springs was anchored in it. It was the only school for all the students in the area. In this building we completed all twelve years of our public schooling, and there intellect was nurtured.

Living in a tiny house with eight other children was bearable but not pleasant or comfortable. The schoolhouse, however, was comfortable. It was warm. It had a library. It smelled like a school, that awful and wonderful aroma I still relish. I savored both the smell and the feel of that old building. It was my haven. I loved the place.

The Great Depression was, in some ways at least, a good time for education. Any job was a prized possession, and a job as a schoolteacher was one of the top prizes. Those who taught there were selected from among many who aspired to do so. My school in Lava Hot Springs was staffed by wonderful teachers. It was small and in many ways limited, but it was the center of learning and culture in the small community where I lived the first eighteen years of my life.

When my senior year in high school came along, my mother had succeeded in her long campaign to get me to make the impossible happen. I was going to leave Lava Hot Springs for college. Her constant advice was that I should present myself in a college registration line and see what happened. If I did that, "things will work out some way or another." My mother had told me this too many times for me to believe otherwise.

Since we had no money at all, I was compelled to attend Albion State Normal School, a teachers training institution, but my love of my hometown school made it easy for me to accept that necessity. If I could make it, I was going to be a teacher. So I hoped as I labored, full of doubts and fearful of the possibility of failure.

To want what may not be attainable and to yearn for opportunity may not be worse for a youngster than to have most wants satisfied and to have boundless clear opportunities. In this sense my twelve years in a one-building school system and my first two years of higher education in a remote state normal school may have been as advantageous to me as the experience of others who attended exclusive, richly endowed private schools and Ivy League universities.

Albion Normal's faculty were not renowned scholars, but they were reasonably bright. It seemed clear to me that they loved their work and respected the students enrolled in their classes. Institutions of uncertain quality and standing must strive to prove their worth. One way this can be done is through the intellectual competence shown by the students who ultimately move on to more prestigious colleges and universities, where they validate the quality of the instruction previously received. In this sense I judge Albion Normal to be more than vindicated.

My life at Albion opened richnesses beyond anything I ever imagined. I was ignorant of our own history and of the great literature of the Western world. I knew nothing of the Federalist Papers, the works of Tolstoy, or the rudiments of economics. This all came to me courtesy of the taxpayers who founded and supported a state normal school to prepare teachers to teach their children and grandchildren. It came courtesy of President Roosevelt's New Deal and the Congress of the United States, which enacted the laws that provided me with a National Youth Administration (NYA) part-time job at a salary of seventeen dollars per month— indispensable to my access to higher education.

Each term I attended seemed likely to be my last. My borrowed textbooks, threadbare clothing, skimpy meals, and constant apprehensiveness that I was not college material caused me—indeed drove me—to study with a dogged passion and urgency.

Having will is as important as being genetically endowed with intelligence and other talents. To reach our outer limits we must have fire in our bellies, or at least under our tails. The will must be strong and relentless. The passion to achieve may be more difficult to sustain in a privileged environment. The problem of American education is akin to the great concern for the future of America itself. How do we keep wide awake on a full stomach?

My life would have been a great void had it not been for that public school in Lava Hot Springs staffed by caring teachers who treasured their jobs. From them I learned that I could learn. I learned as well that the joy of understanding surpasses all else.

Both my public school and Albion State Normal School have been closed. The schoolhouse has been razed, and the campus at Albion, Idaho, is a haunted place. The windows of the buildings have been boarded up, and weeds, brush, and rodents populate the once-green lawns and neatly pruned trees.

To visit either of these sites of my intellectual beginnings is now a painful experience. But to think about the opportunities they provided me is to renew my faith in my testimony that these tax-supported institutions represent the highest of all investments of taxpayers' dollars. My personal story of the Lava Hot Springs public school and Albion State Normal School can be duplicated in the lives of hundreds of thousands across America.

To look into a test tube, to marvel for the first time at a chemical reaction swirling around before your eyes in an Erlenmeyer flask in a public school chemistry laboratory, is to describe the experience that is at the heart of the nation's commitment to the doctrine of life, liberty, and the pursuit of happiness. *We can't promise happiness. But we must promise the pursuit.* My new appointment as Ronald Reagan's Secretary of Education gave me a chance to stand up once again for these ideas.

In Idaho in the late thirties and early forties, our rural schools were staffed by teachers who had attended our two-year normal schools. I did not know that when I was a high school senior, or when I went to Albion State. But Albion State Normal School admitted students for tuition and fees totaling $11.50 per term. That was the place for me because the price was the absolute lowest. So I went to a normal school not knowing that all you could study was teacher education, yet this ignorance brought me to my career in education and ultimately to President Reagan's cabinet.

I was not only promised the pursuit, I was enabled to fulfill it.

I hitchhiked halfway to college and rode a bus the other half because I did not have the funds to pay a full bus fare and the tuition. Albion State Normal turned out to be a dynamic little school. As my mother predicted, "things worked out." The NYA job was made for poverty-stricken students like me. The seventeen dollars per month paid my four dollars monthly rent and left thirteen dollars for food. I scratched out an existence. Every Wednesday my mother sent four loaves of home-made bread in the mail. (The ladies in the Albion post office could smell it through the wrapping.) The big family vegetable garden yielded home-canned vegetables that came to Albion by means of any vehicle that might be heading my way.

Textbooks were my real problem. To buy a book was beyond me. I was a book predator. If I needed to study biology, I walked around the library tables to spy a student reading one text while the biology book I needed (but could not own) sat idle at his or her elbow. I would read until the student had to leave. Then I would reluctantly give back the book and prowl around for another.

Albion Normal required one course in music appreciation and a similar course in art. The wonderful sounds of a Beethoven symphony—the first I had ever heard—overwhelmed me. A magnificent instructor taught me just enough to hunger for more in subsequent years.

A beautiful woman with grace and poise taught me to speak and to write and to read something besides old discarded Street and Smith's *Wild West Weeklies*. That school crammed so much into two years that I felt myself transformed, eager to develop my mind and refine my values. Albion State had a strong commitment to the liberal arts and the humanities. It had had years of experience with rough, crude, and naive students from the Idaho mountains. The pressure was gentle, but it was also steady and carefully meted out to test and lead me to the outer limits of my ability.

History came to life under the guidance of an alcoholic professor who had found refuge in this small country normal school after having been dismissed from a distinguished university in Pennsylvania for drunkenness. He struggled with his problem with the bottle. On more than a few occasions the blackboard displayed his shaky hand: "No class today." Then he would sit in a stupor as we all came in, read the notice, and left. But sober or partially intoxicated, he was an extraordinary teacher. I was exhilarated by his lectures and the new horizons he opened before my wondering eyes. History was tied to current affairs. Editorial pages in newspapers and periodicals became familiar and exciting. He inspired his students to read, to think, and to be active participants in government.

Despite his tragic weakness, he touched my life and sharpened my understanding. When the school administration started to criticize him and press for his dismissal, the students rose up in his defense. We all knew he was a better professor even when half drunk than some others when they were sober. He loved his students and his subject matter. His students understood, and they loved him equally.

The world of science and the marvels of a small laboratory stimulated my interest in physics and chemistry. A clever professor taught us to discover the fundamentals through an inquiry method that kept us in the lab for hours into the darkness. I developed an understanding and appreciation for the scientific method. A new world was revealed to me, and I gained a passion and respect for science that have lasted a lifetime.

Without the NYA's $17 per month and Albion's $11.50 per term bargain-basement tuition, I would have missed the marvelous world of books, libraries, intellectual excitement, and all that is learning beyond high school. This grubby little school with its inconsequential name had high standards, an atmosphere of creative tension, and a remarkably able faculty. It provided a passageway to further learning by disciplining my mind, shaping my values, and raising my self-esteem. Hundreds of small unknown colleges and universities—both public and private—touch the lives of thousands today just as Albion Normal touched mine. As the new Secretary of Education, I knew that I would have the great privilege as well as the solemn obligation to represent all that they do for the United States to the President, his cabinet, and the Congress.

In the middle of my second year at Albion, the Japanese bombed Pearl Harbor. I finished my sophomore courses and enlisted in the United States Marines.

My newly acquired erudition led me into trouble in Marine Corps boot camp. In my last term at Albion I had completed a course in educational tests and measurements, and I was an instant expert at appraising the IQs of all whom I met. One day, as I was picking my teeth in the Marine Corps base theater after leaving the mess hall, I blew a tiny sliver of wood off my lip.

"Spittin' on the floor, eh, Mac?" was the accusation of the MP who was pacing up and down the theater aisle. Using my new powers to measure intelligence, I told the MP he would score no higher than a moron on the Stanford-Binet IQ test. He ushered me before the officer of the day, to whom I expressed my appraisal of the MP's intelligence once more.

The next morning I went before the commanding officer and offered some unsolicited advice on how to improve the entire Marine Corps. The CO was so impressed with my newly acquired Albion Normal School vocabulary that he allowed me to think things over for seventy-two hours in the brig. To relieve my mind of any burdens during my intellectual retreat, they shaved my head, stripped me down to my underwear, and whacked me over the rump and shoulders with rubber hoses as I passed my hosts and keepers along a dark corridor to solitary confinement. Then and thereafter the Marines taught me some lessons I never had at Albion or in Lava Hot Springs.

For three days, I ate bread and drank stale water and relieved myself in a crock in the corner of a very black cell. I sat there, an angry, bitter, undisciplined young man who needed some shock treatment to prepare me for military life. Those three days in total darkness on bread and water seemed like an eternity.

When I came out into the daylight, the newspapers announced another defeat at the hands of the Japanese in the Pacific. "Good news!" I cried to myself in my bitterness.

My years of near-compulsory participation in football (virtually required because our small high school needed every able bodied male out for the team) and my long struggle with the family cow gave me the stamina to cope with three and a half years in the Pacific with the Marines in World War II. Small and runty, I had learned to be feisty. This helped in encounters that led to promotions up the enlisted ranks to first sergeant.

The Marines fought the remainder of World War II without another word of advice from me as to how they might improve their operations. As my mind ran over this, now that I was a newly appointed member of the cabinet, I wondered if Secretary of Defense Cap Weinberger would mind some help in shaping up the Marines!

My rambling thoughts and nostalgic memories were interrupted by the shrill ring of the Mayflower Hotel telephone. It was Pennington James, soon to be the White House assistant to the president for personnel. He had a message from the Commander in Chief of all the Armed Forces as well as the Marines I had been thinking about so deeply. The President-elect wanted to be certain that Utah Republican Senators Garn and Hatch knew of his decision about my appointment. Would I please slip quietly and unnoticed up to the Hill to tell them? The President-elect still wanted to hold the news until 2 P.M. tomorrow, so please be sure to ask the Senators to respect that deadline. We didn't want them to blabber the news early, and we didn't want them angry at us by reading it first in the newspapers.

The reality of the day chased away the reminiscences. I slipped on shoes, necktie, and jacket to catch a cab up to the Senate Office Building. It might be heady stuff to be a newly appointed cabinet member, but I had to win Senate confirmation within a few short days. Without it my tenure would be brief indeed.

Both Utah senators congratulated me on my appointment and promised their support of my confirmation in the Senate. They also promised to obey the Reagan request that they respect the release time of 2 P.M. the next day.

The following morning the *Washington Post* carried the story of my appointment on the front page along with an old photo used back in my years in the Nixon-Ford administrations. So much for Ronald Reagan's desire to keep the news of the appointment under strict wraps until 2 P.M. that afternoon. It was a mystery to me how the story got out, but it was not the first or the last time that such a thing happened in Washington.

CHAPTER 2

Swearing In

‖‖

Foggy Bottom was the scene of the first meeting of Ronald Reagan's cabinet. It was an unofficial session because we met on January 8, 1981, before any of us had taken our oath of office. Shortly before 9 A.M. we gathered in Room 1107 of the main State Department headquarters building. Secretary of State–designate Alexander Haig made the arrangements to host us in the building that was destined to be the scene of his short and tempestuous tenure as the senior cabinet officer. But on that day Al was a gracious host who appeared to be on good terms with the California gang.

The purpose of that first meeting was to teach us about the Ronald Reagan policies that we were expected to implement. The master of ceremonies who made introductions and the preliminary remarks on the topics to be treated by the speakers was Counselor to the President Edwin Meese. Ed carried this responsibility for the entire four years of the president's first term.

The new cabinet members and new White House senior staff stood around drinking coffee and chatting for a brief time. I entered the room feeling somewhat awkward and uncertain. Since I knew only Cap Weinberger and had only a brief acquaintance with Ed Meese and Penn James, I was uneasy about joining any of the conversation groups.

Raymond Donovan, the new secretary of labor, seemed to share my predicament. We introduced ourselves as we looked about the large room to find where our seating assignments were to be. Ray was dressed in a tweed sport jacket and slacks. The rest of us were in dark suits with white shirts and ties. Ray expressed his dismay at guessing wrong about what to wear. I knew from my earlier experiences in Washington that the press watches the new cabinet and their wives. The style section of the *Post* loves to call attention to what it considers dowdy wives and cabinet officers in rumpled clothes. I agreed it was best to play it safe in this town, at least for the first few weeks, and during the lunch break he left to change clothes.

Ed Meese called us together at 9 sharp. We were assigned seats around a U-shaped table. The speakers and senior White House staff sat at a separate table placed at the open end of the U.

As I seated myself where I found my place card, I saw a leather-bound binder with my name and cabinet position stamped in gold letters on the table before me. The realization that I was indeed attending my first cabinet meeting hit me then, making me aware that I was a small part of history being made. I pulled a pen out of my pocket and began to write careful notes on a yellow legal-size pad. Most of what follows is taken from those, notes dated January 8, 1981.

Ed Meese gave us an agenda and made some opening comments. He told us that this would be only the first in a series of "executive seminars." This proved to be a naive expectation. Under the pressures that followed we never held another executive seminar during my four years in the cabinet. We had regular cabinet meetings and cabinet breakfasts but no more so-called executive seminars. He called for a "free and frank discussion." But I noted that the press was present and knew from my past Washington experience that this would be a showplace session, greatly restrained until the press left.

Meese used the word *teamwork* over and over. It seemed redundant to me to tell us we were "part of the President's team." We were his cabinet, so this was obvious. Then Ronald Reagan slipped quietly into the room, followed by Vice President Bush, and Ed introduced the president-elect.

Reagan gave his newly selected cabinet members their first instructions. He told us that our country needed a change. He vowed to press for the program on which he campaigned. He hit several times on the theme that we must "operate as a single unit." He went on to tell us how essential it was to get competent people into the top spots in our departments. He stressed that we needed people who were loyal and who were "real achievers."

He then promised that each secretary would have "full access" to the president. Every cabinet member would either be chairman or a member of groups that would consider issues before they came to the full cabinet and to him for decision. The non-cabinet agencies would also be part of some of these "groups."

Like Meese, Reagan placed considerable emphasis on our being "one team." He told us we would succeed or fail according to how effectively we functioned as "one team." I now wondered if all the emphasis on teamwork was public oratory for the press. I also began to have doubts about the amount of autonomy we would enjoy.

At this point the press was excused. At last we would get down to more substance.

What followed was a presidential warning about the federal bureaucracy and career civil servants. He admonished us that "they" would think the departments were "theirs." He told us to make it plain that we could and would do things differently. We must work hard to manage the civil service bureaucrats. They had been totally unresponsive in the past, and he urged us to "shape them up" early or we would not make the progress he urgently required.

He told us he was going to put a freeze on all hiring. He planned to reduce the size of the bureaucracy by attrition, though he was willing to grant us all an exception to the hiring freeze for those we felt "are needed because they have unique talents that we need."

Ronald Reagan intended to have his cabinet function much like the board of directors of a corporation. He wanted the cabinet to deliberate and offer advice prior to action by the President. In my experiences during the Nixon-Ford years I heard complaints about less and less cabinet involvement in decision making at the White House. In years past, the longer the term of the president, the greater the interval between cabinet meetings. Thus, I didn't believe the promises would last very long and listened to this with skepticism; but in my four years, the President did indeed use his cabinet in the way he described that day.

Next, he promised that we were not going to discuss the political ramifications of either decision making or the outcome of such decisions. We were to "operate like there is not going to be a next election."

Finally, he touched on some lesser matters, such as suggestions about the "cabinet officer quarters." We were not to "redo" our offices, other than to "touch up or to patch a hole in the carpet." He would prefer that we refrain from remodeling them. He emphasized, however, that he did not consider changing the photograph of the president on the wall redecorating.

At this point Reagan told us he had to catch an Air Force plane back to California, but it was a leisurely leave-taking. He paused at the door to tell us that he wanted us to know that he did not expect us to be "rubber stamps." "Let's hear the issues," he said. "I don't need yes men."

He repeated that the government had been "too intrusive" and had been taking too much of the gross national product. How to change this was going to be the subject matter of a big debate.

Finally he told us a couple of stories that I was destined to hear more than once. Then he was gone, and the meeting was left in the hands of his subordinates.

Ed Meese introduced Vice-President George Bush. I took to him at once. He was attractive, poised, and articulate. His experience, warmth, and personal charisma came across to all of us. Here was a very impressive man.

Bush gave us some sage advice about the Washington scene. He told us to beware of "leaks"; giving out information on a confidential basis often led to trouble. Like all his advice, this reflected the experience of his years in public office.

He covered a wide range of subjects. He stressed the importance of seeking out highly qualified women, blacks, and Hispanics for positions of importance in our administration. He advised us on working well with Congress and about responding to their mail and phone calls promptly. He cautioned against "taking positions just to please someone," but it was very important to build support and to be sensitive to the needs of the senators and representatives.

Bush's comments were brief but to the point. His was the most telling presentation I was to hear all day. I liked the leadership qualities and intelligence I heard and could see why Ronald Reagan had selected him to be his vice president.

Senate Majority Leader Howard Baker was introduced next. He, too, was articulate and personable. He needed our help to get the President's legislative program through the Senate. (I was to learn later that Howard's enthusiasm for the president's legislative program did not extend all the way to abolishing the Department of Education.) He promised to help us as cabinet members and urged us to work closely with him and his staff. Our Republican majority in the Senate presented an opportunity and an advantage we must utilize fully.

The Republican minority leader in the House, Congressman Robert Michel, spoke next. I had worked closely with Bob Michel during the Nixon years, when he was the ranking Republican on the Education Appropriations Subcommittee. He was a very able, sincere, and dedicated leader. He warned us that his work would be difficult since Democrats held such a large majority in the House. He told us we would have to make trades and bargain with great skill to get the President's legislative program passed. But we could also take advantage of the conservative Democrats, who were largely from the South. He felt that alliances could be formed with them if we worked carefully to woo the Southern vote away from the Speaker and his leadership team. But the task would be hard. "Every day we will be fifty-one votes short in the House to pass the President's legislation even if all Republicans vote with us."

Michel stressed the need to raise the debt ceiling by February 15 because of the Carter administration's scandalous spending with no concern for the deficit. (At that first cabinet meeting none of us dreamed that we would be running annual deficits in excess of $200 billion over the next few years!) He also told us all to bear in mind that all tax bills had to originate in the House.

The Republican minority leader ended his lecture to the new cabinet by inviting us to meet with him often. "We need the latitude and the opportunity to talk good gut politics," he said.

Then we were introduced to James A. Baker III, the White House chief of staff. Baker was articulate and concise. He talked about organization, operations, and administrative procedures and described the "White House complex." He had 351 employees, half of them career civil servants. This number did not include an additional 1,706 employees of the Executive Office of the President who were not considered White House staff. He wanted to reduce their number by at least 15 percent.

Jim Baker said that past trends had been to centralize control at the White House. He wanted to reverse this and restore more power to the cabinet. His warning that we should expect some "reasonable parsimony" was the understatement of the day.

He listed "four basic aims":

1. To make it possible for each cabinet member to have the right of access to the president
2. To carry out his role as an "honest broker" to see that all who had a right to "have a say" would express that right before final decisions were made
3. To recognize and harmonize views when there were "overlapping interests" and functions among cabinet members
4. To carry out his role to assist the president and to assist each and every member of the cabinet

He outlined what we had to accomplish in the first ninety days of the new administration. First of all, we must get the tax reductions the president had promised the electorate. Then, we must review all federal regulations and cut out all rules and restraints that exceeded the minimum mandated in the statutes. We must push through Congress legislation that would reduce spending. We must simplify and consolidate overlapping or duplicating legislation. And last, we must shrink the size of the federal bureaucracy and use the private sector for more government services where that was feasible. (At this point Jim Brady, the president's press secretary, broke in to admonish us that the "ninety-day goals should not be mentioned out of this room.")

Finally, we were instructed that all paperwork should flow through Jim Baker's office. I was impressed. He gave us valuable and practical information, and he displayed a keen, articulate mind in the process.

We were also introduced to Elizabeth Dole, assistant to the president for public liaison; to Martin Anderson, chief of the Office of Policy Development; to Peter McCoy, administrative head of the First Lady's staff; and to Max Friedersdorf, assistant to the president for congressional relations. Friedersdorf called for regular Friday meetings with our departmental chiefs for legislation.

After these introductions, Penn James led an extensive discussion about appointment procedures. From this exchange I discovered that I had veto power over any appointments proposed for my department. This information proved to be the most important thing I learned from my first meeting with Ronald Reagan, his cabinet, and his senior White House staff, invaluable in my subsequent struggle with right-wing ideologues who wanted to stack the Department of Education with "the right kind of people."

The final discussion centered on the "best and most tactful way" to remove the Carter appointees from office so we could get "our team on board." (This turned out to be no problem for me, for the former president's staff seemed as eager to leave as we were to remove them.)

After a quick briefing by Ed Meese about details of the inauguration events planned for the next few days, the first meeting of the cabinet was adjourned with the expectation that we would have several more orientation sessions. The demands on all our time made this impossible. The full weight of the huge and cumbersome federal establishment was being shifted to our shoulders so rapidly that we had no time to be trained. We learned that in the school of very hard knocks over the next few months of 1981.

The days between our only orientation meeting and the formal inauguration of the president on January 20th, were harrowingly busy. Since I was the last cabinet member selected, my preparation time for taking over my department was extremely short.

Each of the cabinet departments had a transition team that had been studying the immediate problems and the key issues that the department would be facing. The Department of Education transition team briefed me on their findings and recommendations, but they had to deal with a secretary who had been wrestling with the flu and left his sickbed to meet with them. I was hit at a time when I could ill afford to miss a single hour of work, I had worked when I should have been in bed, my strength slipped away, and I finally had to give in to the demands of the bug.

My illness no doubt helped make me impatient and short tempered, but in addition some of the recommendations I heard in my briefing were absolutely ludicrous. I knew, for example, that career civil servants could not be dismissed at the will of a cabinet secretary. Neither could we abolish agencies within our departments that were established by law. Nor could or should we cut out federal financial assistance to students who had been struggling to make their way in our society. My meeting with the transition team was a testy one. I was not prepared to do much of the aggressive abolishing and slashing proposed in its reports.

I was better, though still weak, the Sunday prior to Inauguration Day, when Ronald Reagan invited his cabinet and their wives to church. Betty had flown in from Salt Lake City to participate with me in the official functions, and I appreciated having her by my side at the church services. These were the first non-Mormon church services we had ever attended together. We responded to the beautiful music and an inspiring sermon.

January 20, 1981, was a clear but bone-chilling day. The new president, vice president, and cabinet members officially took the reins of government as Ronald Reagan and George Bush were each sworn in on the west steps of the Capitol.

Following the lead of Chief Justice Warren Burger, the president took the traditional oath: "I, Ronald Reagan, do solemnly swear that I will faithfully execute the office of President of the United States, and will to the best of my ability preserve, protect, and defend the Constitution of the United States." Betty and I were seated behind the podium where the oath of office was administered. The president gave a succinct inaugural address, written on January 8 on nine sheets of lined, yellow legal paper. The president singled out inflation as being the problem "which threatens to shatter the lives of millions of our people." He concluded his address by emphasizing, "We are too great a nation to limit ourselves to small dreams." The twenty-minute address stirred the listeners, and there was a long, standing ovation.

The music, the twenty-one-gun salute, and the pageantry that touched the thousands gathered before us on the great Mall stretching to the Washington Monument. Now the Reagan administration was officially in charge of the executive branch of the United States government. What a moment, I thought. Here I was as a member of the new president's cabinet! As I sat, moved deeply by the powerful historic panorama before me, memories of past experiences in the city came back in full force.

As I sat in my seat during the inauguration ceremony a chill ran through me. It was a physical chill because the cold was already beginning to cause my flu-weakened body to shiver. But it was also an emotional chill, for I had had a bird's-eye view from Capitol Hill of the scene of inevitably rough-and-tumble political warfare and bureaucratic infighting. I knew what was ahead for me. Great tension and rivalry would soon flow up Pennsylvania Avenue from the bowels of the White House, the Old Executive Office Building, and the complex of other offices of the headquarters of the executive branch. Rebuttals, harsh attacks, and even insults would flow back down this historic old street from the ambitious lawmakers. Many aspired to sit in the Oval Office. It was a beautiful, ugly, sick, and lovely scene all wrapped together. I was back in Washington, I realized, with all its emotions: duplicity, chicanery, honor, commitment, genuine patriotism, and, above all, unendurable tensions.

My mind was in a swirl. The intensity of my feelings caused tears to well up into my eyes. As a member of the Reagan cabinet I would be expected to support the president. He was the one elected to office. I hoped to be able to win my point of view on issues before they become administration policy, but whether or not I succeeded, my obligation was to support the President. The nation's schools and colleges were crucial to all that was so powerfully symbolized before me in this historic inaugural scene. What was I going to be able to do for this magnificent, troubled, and criticism-torn education system that encompassed 30 percent of the population of the United States—the students and employees of all the public and private institutions of learning, from kindergarten through graduate school? This was the responsibility before me—to serve and lead and advocate to the man in the Oval Office when we met in the West Wing of the White House, to persuade and teach and guide as best I could.

Would Ronald Reagan endorse what must be done for the learning society that America must become if it is to survive and achieve its destiny? Would I be able to persuade him? My days ahead were going to be filled with agony, tears, frustration, and a few shining moments.

Throughout the inauguration ceremony, I was filled with forebodings of what lay ahead.

After the inauguration, congressional leaders hosted the traditional luncheon in the Capitol. Betty and I sat at a table with Carl Perkins of Kentucky, chairman of the House Education and Labor Committee. My Mormon wife and Chairman Perkins had a friendly exchange about tobacco. Carl told Betty that smoking was harmless and much of the warnings against it hysterical propaganda. I signaled Betty that this was no time to debate a lawmaker from a tobacco state about the harmful effects of smoking. We ended our luncheon on a pleasant and cheerful note and were off to the inaugural parade.

The members of the cabinet were the first on display along the parade route down Pennsylvania Avenue to the presidential viewing stand just outside the White House grounds. Each of us was seated in a separate white Cadillac and chauffeured down the avenue. We went in order of rank. First was Secretary of State Alexander Haig, and thirteenth and last, of course, was Terrel Bell.

Much to my surprise, our limousines were driven swiftly along the parade route. I had thought we would proceed at a slower, more stately parade speed so the viewers could see us. Then I remembered the windows in buildings on either side and the numerous opportunities they offered for snipers.

We ended up in the White House grounds, where we disembarked and mounted a large, open reviewing stand facing a huge bank of television cameras located across the street. Since we were in public view to the entire nation through the miracle of television, it had been suggested that we conduct ourselves with dignity and pay close attention to our appearance.

My military aide had suggested that I not wear my navy blue topcoat because of the television cameras. I complied with his suggestion reluctantly. I erroneously thought that President and Mrs. Reagan would not be permitted to sit in the cold and that radiant electric heaters would keep the temperature tolerable for us all. But the heat was minimal, and we sat out in the frigid January air waiting for the president for what seemed an eternity. We learned later that he had stayed on the telephone in the Capitol, negotiating the terms of the final release of the American hostages who had been held for so many months in our Teheran embassy after it was taken over by Iranian forces. At last he arrived and the parade proceeded.

The final float was the world-renowned Mormon Tabernacle Choir carried on a huge flatbed truck. The choir stopped before the presidential party and sang the "Battle Hymn of the Republic." The choir had a special meaning for us, and the music was stirring. Then the parade was over and the shivering grandstand watchers welcomed the opportunity to go indoors and to complete the day with a few more ceremonial events.

The Senate approved my appointment as U.S. secretary of education three days after the inauguration. I was sworn in at the White House along with three other cabinet members. There was no ceremony, and there were no witnesses other than a few White House staffers. We stood in a room together, raised our right hands, and repeated the oath. I signed the required papers. I was now lawfully installed.

The next major milestone was the president's State of the Union message to Congress and to the people of the United States. This is required by law, and the first *state of the union* address of a new president is particularly significant because the new administration makes its recommendations to Congress and generally outlines in detail what it plans to accomplish.

The days immediately following the president's inauguration were filled with activity related to the content of this address. Each cabinet member was invited to comment and give input on aspects of the speech that related to his or her particular area of responsibility, and several drafts of the speech crossed my desk. But this presented little challenge to me, unhappily, for there was nothing of significance to education in the president's first State of the Union address.

And then came the ignominy of my being designated the cabinet member to stay home and watch the proceedings on television. As the cabinet member's faces appeared on the network TV screens, my absence was noted. I had several inquiries from colleagues in education leadership positions and from friends and relatives back home. Several small but humorous items appeared in newspapers and news magazines. It gave journalists an opportunity to note once again that my position was on the Reagan chopping block. I didn't need reminding.

CHAPTER 3

The Great New Beginning Begins

||||||||||||||||||||||||||||||||||||||||||||||||||||||||||||||||||||||||||||||||||||||||||||||||||||||||||||||||||||||||||||||||||||||||||||||||||||

Question: **"Who's that white-haired gentleman in the brown suit?"**
Answer: **"A gentleman does not wear a brown suit—unless he's from Kansas!"**

My hair is white. I was wearing a brown suit. The above conversation was overheard at a reception for new cabinet members and other presidentially appointed officials of the Reagan administration.

Not only do I like brown suits, I have a special affinity for Kansas and an antipathy for stuffed shirts. This exchange mirrored the natural and sometimes cynical curiosity of the permanent Washington establishment as they picked at the new officialdom of the Reagan government.

I received more than my share of the misanthropic probing into origins and qualifications because I was the last cabinet member appointed, and it had been well publicized that my only assignment was to abolish the Department of Education and go home. Indeed, one of the early cartoons that enjoyed wide play in the nation's press depicted the empty cabinet room with labels on each chair around the table. The one for the secretary of education down at the end of the room was an electric chair.

In the minds of business executives, educators are notoriously bad managers. They aren't very bright, and when it comes to intestinal fortitude they are totally gutless. Unfortunately, one does not have to look very long to find a few members of our species who eloquently prove this point. Still, I doubt we have any more duds per hundred than those found in the business community. The label certainly does not belong on all of us. It is prejudice—prejudgment—not unlike the other bigotries that place all members of a group under the same labels. The biased observer finds one Hispanic who is not very ambitious so all Mexican

Americans are labeled lazy. All Indians walk single file; at least the one I saw did. This was a presumption with which I had to contend at the outset of my term in office. I was an educator, so there were labels on me from the day I took office. There wasn't much I could do about it.

The Reagan cabinet was examined by the *Washington Post,* the *Washington Star,* the *New York Times, Newsweek, Time, U.S. News & World Report,* the major wire services, the three major TV networks, and by other eminent newspapers and periodicals. Press comment on my appointment was almost totally negative. The traditional conservative press, such as *Human Events* and *National Review,* expressed consternation and dismay. As I have noted, the *Wall Street Journal* said that the president had selected a very distinguished cabinet, up to his final choice. Then he had foolishly selected a man from the educational establishment to be his secretary of education.

All of this sounds as though I am having a pity party with myself as the featured guest. My grandfather, who tried to function as a father during my early years, had admonished me not to feel sorry for myself because of my mother's widowhood and our poverty.

"Terrel," he would begin. "The only thing that stinks worse than self-praise is self-pity. Take your lot as it is and go from there."

Politically, I was sitting on death row. I needed to keep my grandfather's warning uppermost in my mind or I could indeed turn despondent.

We took office in late January, and as early as late February and early March I was being nudged to get moving to abolish my department and get out of town. At social events during the get-acquainted era of the president's first term, the keepers of the conservative dogma would exclaim, "My, are you still here?" "Haven't you started to shut down your department?" "Do you need some help on moving expenses?"

This last question was prompted by the fact that the Bell family household goods had been moved to Washington as usual by U-Haul truck. We did not have the cash to employ a moving company. We bought our own packing boxes, packed the belongings we needed for a transient term in Washington, loaded our rented truck, and drove it from Salt Lake City to the nation's capital in the depth of winter. It wasn't a glamorous arrival.

The tenuousness of my position presented a quandary as to choice of residence. Betty and I finally decided to rent rather than buy. We wanted to be close to the city, and we needed a school that would be academically challenging for our youngest son, Peter. We rented a two-bedroom town house in Arlington, Virginia. It had three levels, giving us an opportunity for some added exercise.

Peter registered at Tuckahoe Elementary School. We chose the school prior to finding the house. This turned out to be a very wise choice. The Arlington schools are outstanding in their commitment to academic excellence, and Tuckahoe Elementary School is in our opinion the best of the Arlington family of public schools.

The press had another fling at us in those first few days in our new home. A newspaper reporter came out to see us soon after we moved in. She brought a photographer with her. They interviewed us and inspected and photographed our premises from top to bottom.

The next Sunday we were featured in the life-style section of the *Washington Post*. The article described our plastic-base lamps, and our "dimestore furniture." The article located our residence as "overlooking the Exxon station between Lee Highway and Washington Boulevard." We were still looking for carpet, so the bare floors added to the look of austerity that was so explicitly described in the *Post*.

As the press continued to inspect, search, and peer at the members of the cabinet, the conclusion was that I was a strange fit with the rest. One article claimed that I was the only one who was not a millionaire. With my plastic lamps, brown suits, white hair, bare floors, U-Haul truck, a department characterized before the public as Ed Meese's "great bureaucratic joke," and a ranking thirteenth out of thirteen cabinet secretaries, I was off to an inglorious start. Indeed, there could hardly be a lower status than to be a Republican in the Reagan administration in charge of a department sired by Jimmy Carter, mothered by Congress, delivered by the National Education Association functioning as an activist midwife, and publicly designated for abolition.

Nonetheless, I *was* a member of the president's cabinet. He may have wished he didn't have to have me, but there I was in my seat at the cabinet table by act of the Congress of the United States.

My quick-witted and teasing son, Peter, said to me often in those early days: "Dad, if it weren't for Jimmy Carter, you wouldn't even have your job!" My son's needling didn't hurt; my skin was getting thicker by the day.

We were the new government. We came to office with the authority of law behind us. We were what citizens think of when they speak of their government. We were the officialdom. We would, for a time only, govern because Ronald Reagan had been elected. We would govern by the consent of the governed. But, after four years, we might well be objects of the traditional "Throw the rascals out!"

Aristotle observed that under democratic government individuals may both "rule and be ruled by turns." It was our turn now to rule. Technically, the body of the citizens as a whole may be in charge, but for a specified term we were the ones holding public office and control of the executive branch of our government.

Many of us forget that officeholders in government have two kinds of power. First, they have the legal authority that is theirs by virtue of the office they hold. Second, they have power that can grow or shrink depending on the respect or scorn that they gain while carrying out their responsibilities. This capacity comes from reputation. Politically, therefore, reputation derives from both reality and public perception. It is a product of both performance and posture.

No matter how able an elected public servant may be, the perception of his or her ability in the minds of the voters will determine future capacity to win and hold office. This relates to style. It comes from the performance of the officeholder.

Early in the administration's first months in office, U.S. Army Brigadier General John Dozier was kidnapped by an underground organization in Italy. A ransom was demanded. The president immediately began to work for his release. Labor Secretary Raymond Donovan kiddingly observed that I had better be careful not to get myself kidnapped. "The president won't spend a dime to pay for your release," he told me.

When we gathered in the cabinet room of the West Wing of the White House for our first official cabinet meeting following Inauguration Day I was both apprehensive and curious. I would see Ronald Reagan in his official capacity as he presided over his cabinet. What would this former professional movie actor do? What would his leadership style be? Would he be aggressive and pushy? Would he be laid back and nonassertive? How specific would he be about his program?

My chauffeur displayed his experience and reputation with the White House gate guards and Secret Servicemen responsible for security by taking me into the White House grounds at the Executive Avenue entrance that brought us into the West Wing area. Other cabinet officials and their drivers had to go through some thorough identification, but Charles Holton was so well known and so fully trusted that we were whizzed right past the big iron gates into the parking area between the Old Executive Office Building and the White House West Wing where the president, the vice president, and the senior staff all had their offices.

The White House is a labyrinth of narrow corridors and a tangle of stairs and offices. This is particularly true of the West Wing, where the Oval Office, the cabinet room, the Roosevelt Room, and all the senior staff offices are located. It was a challenge just to find one's way upstairs from the Executive Avenue entrance to the cabinet room.

When I arrived in the cabinet room for our first official meeting, I saw cabinet members crouching down to read something on the backs of the chairs surrounding a large, angular table that filled much of the room. I followed suit, to find that the back of the chair I was peering at bore the designation: Secretary of Housing and Urban Development.

I looked for my chair and found it down at the far side of the table next to the end. These chairs were distanced from the president according to cabinet rank. So, once again, I was in seat thirteen, the greatest distance away from Ronald Reagan. Directly opposite the president sat Vice President Bush. Al Haig, the secretary of state, was on Reagan's right. On the president's left sat Cap Weinberger, the secretary of defense. On the vice president's right sat Donald Regan, secretary of the treasury. On his left was the attorney general, William French Smith. The rest of us were seated in descending order of rank.

The counselor to the president had cabinet rank, so Ed Meese had a seat at one end of the cabinet table, as did David Stockman, director of the Office of Management and Budget. The federal trade representative, William Brock, and the president's chief of staff, James A. Baker, also had seats at the cabinet table.

Down at the other end of the table were seats for two others who held cabinet rank but were not cabinet officers and were not successors to the presidency in the statutory order of succession. These seats belonged to William Casey, director of the Central Intelligence Agency, and Jeane Kirkpatrick, U.S. ambassador to the United Nations.

The president came in, flanked by Ed Meese and Jim Baker. We immediately stood up to show our respect.

"Don't get up," Reagan admonished us. "We'll be doing this regularly and you don't need to stand up." But each time during the four years that I served in his cabinet we always stood when he entered. We respected the office, but we also respected the man. That respect continued over the many meetings and through some very trying times.

As the president sat down, he reached over to the center of the table to pull a large jar of jelly beans his way. He selected jelly beans from the jar and then passed it on to Cap Weinberger.

I hate jelly beans. Here was another small token of my not fitting in. As the jar came around, each cabinet member selected a few beans. I decided then and there that I wouldn't eat those sugary, sticky morsels just to be in step with the others. I simply slid the jar on to Richard Schweiker, the secretary of health and human services.

The chair I occupied was bulky, heavy, and uncomfortable. I am very short, as I've noted. If I stretch I may measure five feet five inches in height. Thus, my legs wouldn't touch the floor if I sat back in the chair. I didn't like jelly beans and my chair didn't fit. Cabinet meetings were apparently not going to be enjoyable for me.

It would be unthinkable to ask for a different chair that would not match the rest. This chair had my date of taking office and my official position engraved on it. It was obvious that I was destined to sit in it, however uncomfortable it was.

I glanced over my shoulder and realized that the famous White House Rose Garden was on the other side of the wall just behind me. Many historic events had been solemnized out there over the years. The light was good, the setting was colorful, and it was an ideal place for posturing before cameras. Posturing being Washington's favorite pastime, this special spot was in heavy demand by both president and the press.

Like other presidents before him, Mr. Reagan selected portraits of favorite presidents to display on the walls of the cabinet room. I noted that he had chosen Calvin Coolidge to occupy the spot to the right of the door he would use each time he came into the cabinet room from the Oval Office. He displayed a portly William H. Taft to the left of this door. Opposite my seat hung portraits of Abraham Lincoln and Thomas Jefferson. Over the mantel of the fireplace at the end of the room where I sat we could view the countenance of Dwight D. Eisenhower.

The staff kept the president supplied with water. Thirst apart, frequent drinks of water help keep the plumbing flushed out for those with prostate irritation. In subsequent cabinet meetings I noted that other members had ordered water. Ours was not a youthful group, and I smiled to myself as they joined the water gang.

The president launched right into the business at hand. We had gone to church with Ronald Reagan twice before his inauguration, so I had expected an invocation before he started his cabinet meetings. Both the Senate and the House of Representatives begin each day with prayers in their chambers. The U.S. Supreme Court does too. Since the president had stumped for prayer in the schools during his election campaign, it surprised me that he chose not to follow the practice of the other two branches of government.

In this and subsequent cabinet meetings I learned to admire Ronald Reagan's leadership style. His sessions started on time. The schedule indicated when we would conclude. He focused on the specified agenda, and he dismissed us promptly. It was obvious that he was an effective executive. It didn't take long for him to win the respect of everyone who sat at the cabinet table.

I soon learned that the president liked anecdotal information that illustrated needs, problems, and potential solutions. He frequently drew on his California experiences. Indeed, as I have mentioned, we heard some stories more than once. But he was not one to ramble on, and in my four years of constant contact and observation I never detected any evidence of mental decline. His mind was sharp, and he was well tuned to the issues discussed.

David Stockman, in his book *The Triumph of Politics,* claimed that the president wandered in circles on policy matters, not giving direction with respect to decision making. I never saw evidence of this. He often made decisions on budget and other matters that I did not like, some of which made me angry. But I never felt that his policies were aimless or wandering or lacked clear focus. Like most politicians, he compromised and accepted less than he wanted from time to time. Conservative critics sneeringly call this pragmatism. But compromise is the essence of political effectiveness; he would have been an ineffective president if he had not known when to compromise and when to hold fast. Ronald Reagan made decisions that David Stockman did not like. Maybe this was the source of Dave's complaints that Reagan did not give direction. The direction was the president's, and from time to time it did not accord with Dave's. Reagan was a decisive leader, and it is inaccurate to portray him otherwise.

I also noted in our first cabinet sessions that he was a very astute politician. His eight years of experience working with the California legislature helped him to be ready for combat with the Congress.

At the suggestion of Ed Meese, he established a system for cabinet-level examination and discussion of issues that had to come before him for final decision. He set up subunits of the cabinet, called cabinet councils. These groups studied issue papers and alternative actions that might be taken to solve problems. I attended many of these sessions, which were usually steered by Ed Meese. The president wanted our views and his system of cabinet councils was a good way to get them. We prepared for them by spending hours reading books and studying the briefing materials. When we had completed these homework assignments, the president would meet with the group that had been working on a particular problem. "O.K., let's round-table it," he would say. He then listened to the issues and the varied points of view, though he usually made his decisions after the meetings were over.

This procedure, which assured careful deliberation on important issues, was abolished when Donald Regan became chief of staff and Meese left the White House to become attorney general. Had it continued, I believe some serious and painful mistakes would have been avoided during Reagan's second term.

Ronald Reagan made us work. He kept his cabinet councils actively engaged in weighing alternatives and reading and interpreting data provided by lower-level government offices. In this way he could be thoroughly informed without subjecting himself to the impossible burden of countless hours of study late into the night.

In other words, he delegated effectively. He did not get bogged down in details. He had time to evaluate perspectives, to see the picture as a whole. He had time to relax occasionally, riding horses at Camp David, time to be on the telephone and to keep appointments in his office and for the endless process of working with Congress. He worked us hard so he could do his job and still be relaxed. That is the mark of a skillful executive. He knew how to delegate and when to monitor. He had a laid-back style, but this did not mean he was not effective. Indeed, it enabled him to be effective.

He was a thoughtful human being, too. The president remembered the little, personal things that made you like him all the more. He always called me on my birthday. He responded in other caring ways. We appreciated his individual invitations to each cabinet couple up to the private White House residence for dinner.

Given my bias on behalf of education, it was easy for me to be upset at his budget proposals and at some totally wrongheaded initiatives to abolish education programs that were urgently needed by the people. I had to defend some proposals to Congress that were, in my view, absolutely wrong. I did so after I had either lost the arguments or knew that debate would be futile. Given his forcefulness and leadership, it was not surprising that Ronald Reagan made decisions that I didn't like. But, unlike Stockman, I didn't attribute them to lack of direction; in fact, quite the reverse. His personableness and his ability to disarm his critics worked on me as well as on all the others who learned to love the man in spite of his decisions. It is hard not to like Ronald Reagan.

The U.S. Department of Education was created from units that had formerly been attached to the old Department of Health, Education, and Welfare. When I took office in January 1981 the department had only been in existence since the previous May. Federal Judge Shirley

Hufstedler was the first secretary of education. President Carter had fought hard to create the department, and he selected Mrs. Hufstedler to guide the fledgling cabinet agency in its first months. She did an outstanding job of organizing the new department.

In January 1981 the department had a budget in excess of $14,-700,000,000 and a staff of over 7,000 employees. Yet the department did not have a home. Its units were scattered all over the city in sixteen different locations. My office was on the fourth floor of a federal office building that also housed NASA headquarters.

The Department of Education had responsibility for several crucial functions that served the nation's schools and colleges. We allocated federal funds to school districts and colleges, and we were responsible to Congress to see that the educational institutions that claimed the money utilized it under the provisions of law. Like statutes pertaining to other federal programs, education laws enacted by Congress contained more detail and prescriptiveness than I felt was necessary.

Our mission was primarily one of advocating, monitoring, and supporting equal educational opportunity. For example, we allocated over $3.5 billion each year to schools to provide special help to enhance learning for disadvantaged children. This financial assistance had to be allocated to school districts on the basis of the number of low-income children as defined in the law. The funds had to be spent where there were concentrations of these children. They were to supplement what the states and local school districts provided. The law was complex and required a staff of education specialists and auditors to prevent fraud and misuse of funds. We also tried to keep schools informed of new and improved ways to teach the disadvantaged.

Congress also held us responsible for administering a law enacted to guarantee ''free and appropriate education'' for all handicapped children in the United States. This statute, enacted during the Ford administration, came into existence out of testimony given in extensive congressional hearings. Some states and school districts had been excluding from school significant numbers of handicapped children who had learning potential but were difficult to educate. Some of the children were also physically upsetting to look at because of such disabilities as cerebral palsy. These children's rights were being violated, and Congress passed a very tough, appropriately prescriptive law to ensure that these young citizens would have learning opportunities suitable to their needs. Ideally, it would have been a better solution for each of the states to have passed its own provisions for the handicapped. But down through the years a significant number of states never did this, so Congress stepped in to fill the void. An outrageous injustice had to be corrected, and it took federal-level action because of state-level negligence. This statute placed another heavy responsibility on the Department of Education.

In hearings conducted over a period of years, Congress also found that many worthy students were being deprived of the opportunity for a college education because they came from low-income families. The experience with the GI Bill of Rights, enacted at the end of World War II, showed Congress—and the nation—that financial assistance for college education for veterans was an investment of taxpayers' money that yielded many benefits to society, as well as financial dividends in the form of tax revenues returning to the government. Education made taxpayers out of potential tax consumers. (Indeed, like millions of veterans, I myself had been a beneficiary of the GI Bill, returning to Albion State—by then renamed Southern Idaho College of Education—at war's end for my BA, and over subsequent years earning MA and Ph.D. degrees with the welcome aid of grants and fellowships.)

A program of federal financial assistance to students to help them defray the costs of college attendance was enacted. The program has three components. Part time jobs are provided through grants made to colleges. Eighty percent of the cost of these part-time student jobs is paid by the Department of Education. Low-income students in greater need are given Pell grants (named after Senator Claiborne Pell of Rhode Island), funded by the federal government. Students must meet the low-income criteria, and they must make satisfactory progress in their college studies. The third element of the federal assistance program to college students is the guaranteed student loan program. The Department of Education guarantees the repayment of loans and provides interest subsidies on student loans. This program is complex. It involves repayment to banks when students default, aggressive collection action (recently enacted) against loan defaulters, and (in another aspect of the program) campus-based loans made directly by an institution to certain students in special need.

The U.S. Department of Education has a civil rights enforcement arm. This unit was created to enforce laws that prohibit discrimination on the basis of race, ethnic origin, sex, age, or handicapping condition. It is dedicated to the idea of equal opportunity. School desegregation, compulsory busing, and other actions have been ordered by the federal courts. The Department of Education must monitor for compliance, investigate complaints, and see that civil rights laws in education are enforced in thousands of schools and colleges. In our complex nation it is not sufficient to enact laws requiring equal rights and prohibiting discrimination; they must also be enforced, and this was the responsibility of our Office of Civil Rights.

The Department of Education is also responsible for administering the rehabilitation laws for handicapped adults. Additionally, there are bilingual education programs for public school students who cannot write, read, or speak English. Other statutes too numerous and detailed to describe here are also administered by the department.

The department receives funds for research in the field of education. The Nixon administration pushed through Congress an act creating the National Institute of Education (NIE). This was seen as the education research equivalent of the National Institutes of Health (NIH) in the field of health, where rapid advances have been made in medicine and allied areas. A National Center for Education Statistics was also established by Congress. This center gathers data on education that can be used by the Congress, state legislatures, school boards, and colleges; by knowing about the condition of education across the nation, more rational decisions can be made by lawmakers, governing boards, and administrators.

The Department of Education thus has many significant responsibilities to help the states, school districts, colleges, and private schools meet the educational needs of the American people. As with civil rights, the duties of the department are prescribed by law, and the responsibility is fixed on the U.S. secretary of education to see that these laws are faithfully administered.

Many thoughtful citizens believe that education should be the exclusive duty of the states. Congress has come to feel otherwise. The courts have also interpreted the Constitution and the Bill of Rights in a manner that places some responsibility for education on the executive branch of the federal government. The U.S. Department of Education was created to administer laws enacted by the Congress.

.This was the structure and these were the obligations I inherited when I entered on my duties. I took an oath faithfully to perform my responsibilities as secretary of education. I interpreted this oath with more fervor than my critics would have wished, and I could not have done otherwise.

I loved my work. My work had been good to me. It pushed me to put all my heart and soul into what I did. Those who accused me of being part of the educational establishment were right.

People like me who have labored in the teaching and learning vineyard for years form an emotional commitment to students, schools, books, libraries, and academic life in general. It grows on us until it becomes an obsession that takes control of our minds and wills. It is a mild form of insanity.

I came to the position of U.S. secretary of education when this obsession was at its peak. I had been involved in the war against ignorance and neglect for thirty-five years. I knew what would be best for American education, and a cocksure certainty permeated my thinking. As I criticized the extreme positions taken by the radical right, I knew that I too was a zealot. I was a missionary ready to preach the gospel of education to all the Reaganites.

Alert though I was to the way Washington worked, this mental and emotional commitment made me ill-prepared for what lay ahead as I matched my wit and will with the angry people who just as passionately wanted the government out of education. I listened with alarm to David Stockman's early attacks on student financial aid when we took over the Carter budget and prepared our administration's recommendations for revision. I could not fathom his rationale for the budgetary choice of cutting student aid and retaining such other less worthy expenditures as subsidies for growing cancer-causing tobacco.

What puzzled me the most about Stockman's education funding OMB choices was the emphasis on government handouts in preference to programs such as work-study opportunities and guaranteed loans. Dave was quick to place heavy cuts on the latter and lighter hits on grants that were outright gifts. Having been taught in both church and home to help yourself first, borrow and pay back if you could, and accept charity last, I could never understand the Stockman priority. To my mind, it's always better to help someone help him- or herself than simply to hand over money.

Back in my early years in my small hometown, I was often the recipient of charity. Accepting a handout beats starving, to be sure. But it made me feel ashamed and embarrassed. At least if one can do some work in return for the largesse it helps to build some feelings of self-worth.

When it came time for me to graduate from high school, I was honored to be one of the two valedictorians of my class. This created another source of embarrassment. In our high school in those days we did not wear the now-traditional rented caps and gowns. The young women wore their best dresses. The young men wore dark suits with a white shirt and tie. My problem was that I owned none of these.

I confided in my mother that I needed either to rent a suit or to play sick on graduation day. But to my astonishment she told me that she had the money to buy the appropriate clothing for graduation. This was hard to believe. When I asked how she had come into such unexpected riches, she simply said that she had "raised" the money. So I appeared to give my valedictory address in a new suit with the appropriate white shirt and tie.

Two years later, as I prepared to leave to do my duty in World War II with the U.S. Marines, I finally discovered the source of the money for the clothing. My face turned crimson as I learned that on graduation day I had been on public display before those who had chipped in the money to buy my graduation suit. The faculty of Lava Hot Springs High School had all contributed a portion of their meager salaries to see that their valedictorian was properly attired. Knowing that I would object to this, my mother withheld the information; this accounted for her evasiveness when I asked about the money. She was such a frugal person that I simply assumed that she had been saving for four or five years for this event.

So I had been the recipient of a handout from my own teachers. I had stood before them and my classmates in my new clothing to give my speech. The entire faculty knew that they owned a piece of what I was wearing. The memory of it still makes me blush, and I know at least one of the sources of my strong conviction that when assistance is necessary, it is self-help that leads to independence and pride in oneself.

But neither my concern about fitting into the new cabinet nor my discomfiting encounters with Stockman remained my main concern. Conflicts with the White House Personnel Office and problems surrounding senior staff appointments soon became a bigger threat than OMB.

CHAPTER 4

Staffing Reagan's *Titanic*

‖‖‖

Had it been widely known prior to its first cruise that the *Titanic* was destined to sink, would this have complicated the recruiting chores? My task in attracting quality assistant secretaries at the Department of Education was plagued by the *Titanic* syndrome. All cabinet secretaries struggled with the task of staffing in the first weeks of the new administration, but since my department was to be abolished, the problems of senior staff appointments were obviously more complex.

The president's new cabinet had to get their departments ready to govern. Each of us had to select an undersecretary and a large number of assistant secretaries, each of whom oversaw a specific unit. These units were known as subcabinets. Many of them were large and complex. (The assistant secretary for higher education in the Department of Education, for example, managed billions of dollars of college student financial aid and other programs related to the nation's college and university system.) These were very responsible and often sensitive positions; and, given the critical nature of the programs, I wanted to select leaders on the basis of their qualifications without concern for political ideology.

The president had wisely assured his cabinet that he would not force us to employ senior staff that we did not want. The presidential edict established the setting for a protracted fight over who would serve in the subcabinets of my department. Without this insistent and unwavering position, taken early in the president's term, I would have been immediately surrounded by true believers and I would have been forced out of office in six months. However, I had veto power, and I used it.

White House ideologues urged Personnel Director Pennington James to see that I had the "right kind of people" in the key positions in my department, which they referred to as "ED" in their internal notes and memos that I intercepted through my own White House sources. Ed Meese, during his four years as counselor to the president, prior to his becoming U.S. attorney general, stood out as the keeper of the radical right dogma. The leaders of the extreme right quickly made their way to his West Wing office.

Meese was a confidant of Pennington James. They were longtime friends dating back to the days of Reagan's tenure as governor of California. This close association made it difficult to gain clearance of any candidate who did not meet with Meese's approval, a circumstance that also gave added power to movement conservatives close to Meese.

In my effort to solve this problem of appointment of senior staff, I became acquainted for the first time with these *movement* conservatives. Being a lifelong Republican, I had worked for years with both conservatives and moderates. Those I had known were practical politicians; they would work hard for the outcomes to which they had strong commitments, but they would compromise after they had determined that the results of debate and negotiation represented the best they could expect at that particular time. The movement conservatives were scornful of compromise; and those who did so were labeled "pragmatists." To become a pragmatist by compromising rather than waging a fight to the end was a failure to keep the faith and a sign of weakness and wishy-washy convictions.

This group was almost like a secret society. They looked after each other. They shared horror stories about the rest of us, and I knew they had labeled me as philosophically unfit for a high-level position from the day my appointment was announced. I was not the only one so identified. Meese and his followers looked on George Bush and Jim Baker as pragmatists too.

The movement conservatives closed ranks and vowed to make the time of the Reagan administration a period of revolution. They identified the true members of the movement and distinguished them from conservatives who practiced the art of compromise. These movement people proclaimed their ideological identity on cuff links and neckties. Their logo was the profile of Adam Smith, the author of the classic economic work, *The Wealth of Nations*.

The undersecretary (the number two position in a cabinet department) and all assistant secretaries are presidentially appointed, and their approval requires the advice and consent of the Senate. This situation set the stage for a bitter and protracted fight over the political versus the professional qualifications of the people proposed for these high-level positions.

When candidates for such presidentially appointed posts were under consideration, the movement conservatives would search the record to see who among them were pragmatists and who were solid conservatives with no history of deviating from the movement ideology. In ED, since they had lost the battle to put one of their own in the secretary's chair, the next best thing was to staff all the other senior staff positions with "the right people." This was a difficult goal to achieve because of that effective veto power the president had given his cabinet over appointments in their departments. Nevertheless, the movement's opposition could be formidable, and my problems were enhanced by the general belief that the department was not involved in anything worthwhile anyway. The more we suffered, the sooner we would be willing to concede defeat and fold up the entire unit. Indeed, several newly arrived White House staff members were so ill informed that they actually believed that if I chose, I could unilaterally close the department down, fire all the employees, and bring about the total demise of the federal role in education. Given this kind of naïveté, it was easy for the next scheme to emerge: to bottle up all my proposed appointments and approve only the ideologues.

While we waited and waited for approval of the nominees whose names I had sent the White House Personnel Office, I appointed acting assistant secretaries to fill each vacancy. These came from the career civil service ranks. From my experience as commissioner of education in the old Office of Education (the *E* in HEW) I knew the capacities and weaknesses of many of the executive-level career people. I simply placed the appropriate person in temporary charge. I had decided that I would take my time with the administration-endorsed political appointees. I was not going to commit political suicide. The approval of the extremists being pushed on me would not only cause many difficulties, it would ultimately embarrass the President.

My first effort was to get the number two person in place. The White House proposed Loralee Kinder to be the undersecretary of education. I rejected this. She had served as chair of the transition task force for education, many of whose proposals I vigorously disagreed with. Even more important, she lacked the education credentials to command the necessary respect of the academic community. I proposed the name of Christopher Cross. I was certain that his work as a scholar and leader in education would add to the prestige of the department. He was a Republican as well as a respected educator. I had known Chris from my HEW days during the Ford administration, and knew he would fill the post admirably. White House Personnel, still angered by my veto of Loralee Kinder, quickly rejected Chris Cross.

Chris subsequently wrote a letter to the editor that appeared in the *Washington Post*. He told of his experience as a candidate being courted by a Reagan cabinet member for a presidential appointment, only to be dropped like a hot potato after the rumors of the appointment had been widely circulated and his current employers had come to wonder about his commitment to them. Chris was working for the Westinghouse Learning Corporation, and the public disclosure of his candidacy was embarrassing to him. His letter received prominent play in the press. I could not tell Chris the real story.

Given the size of the federal government and the thousands of appointments to be made in those hectic early days of Reagan's first term, the director of White House Personnel could not personally act on every proposal. This gave second- and third-level staff people in this office power to reject cabinet-level recommendations. The two actions with respect to Loralee Kinder and Chris Cross occurred during that frantic time, when the paperwork and volume of actions were overwhelming.

Nonetheless, the Chris Cross episode is an example of the somewhat cumbersome, time-consuming, and often bizarre circumstances that surround presidential appointments in any administration, Democratic or Republican. The candidate must pass clearance in the political arena. This usually involves approval by the offices of the Republican and Democratic National Committees. This is preceded by a thumbs-up response from the state-level committee of the party. There may also be county-level political checking. All this base-touching has become a tradition because, over the years, political leaders back home have on occasion objected to appointments of those who cannot pass the state and local litmus tests.

After this "clearance," the jockeying between the White House and the cabinet department intensifies. If an agreement is reached, the candidate is then investigated by the Federal Bureau of Investigation. An FBI agent calls at the place of employment, on neighbors in the candidate's residential area, and anywhere else that sensitive information can be obtained. The FBI tries to learn about his or her background, reputation, moral standing, and overall reputation before the President sends the name to the Hill for Senate approval.

When a new administration takes over, the number of FBI background investigations soars, and a sizable backlog builds up. Candidates have to wait their turn. It is often a very long wait. In the meantime, the rumors proliferate and the candidate must have a very strong yearning for the job to withstand the emotional pressure and loss of privacy.

Nor is that all. When the full field investigation is completed, those close to the President and responsible for saving him from embarrassment usually send out trial balloons through the press to see if there will be any unanticipated political fight over the appointment. Often, only after a pending high-level appointment has been flaunted publicly will such opposition surface, despite all the clearances that have preceded it. For example, the heated opposition to Justice Rehnquist's nomination for advancement to chief justice of the Supreme Court came out after the trial ballooning. His ownership of property under possibly racially biased zoning restrictions was placed in the public light of the press. Usually it is only at this point that there are indications of a Senate confirmation fight instead of smooth sailing. This is why "usually reliable sources" are quoted to the effect that so and so is under strong consideration for appointment by the President to X position in his administration. If criticism emerges and the appointment appears to be controversial, the President and his staff will weigh whether the candidate is worth a fight and the expenditure of political capital. It is not uncommon at this late juncture of the tortuous appointment process for the poor soul to be dropped abruptly and without comment. Rumors have flown around in the press. Current employers are aware of the candidacy. The FBI has been busy poking about his or her neighborhood and place of work. Local, state, and national political leaders have been contacted. The consideration is a widely known "secret." To be abandoned after all this is obviously humiliating. It is a wonder our government attracts any talent at all to high positions.

Many outstanding citizens would be willing to respond to a call from the president or from a cabinet officer to serve their country, but they are understandably unwilling to run the gamut of this procedure. The nation loses many of its best qualified potential public servants because of this lengthy and excruciating process of public exposure.

Moreover, even if the candidate hangs in and the appointment is finally announced by the President, he or she must still win the "advice and consent" of the Senate. The trial balloons do not preclude unexpected problems. The opposition party often wants to expose the administration's weaknesses if it can. It digs even further into the candidate's background. It questions in the hearings before the Senate committee as carefully as possible and sometimes for a long, occasionally miserable time.

I served as acting U.S. commissioner of education for seven months in 1970 while the Senate debated the fitness of Dr. Sidney P. Marland, Jr., to serve as U.S. commissioner of education in the old HEW. This was a horrendous experience for Sid Marland, a distinguished educator and one of our genuinely outstanding commissioners of education. It was a miracle that he was still willing to serve—at a salary greatly reduced from his previous position—when the Senate finally gave its consent.

Even under normal circumstances, the selection and ultimate confirmation of a presidential appointee are very difficult, time-consuming, and frustrating for the cabinet officer and the candidate he or she has recruited. But when a fight simmers between the White House staff and a cabinet secretary, the ensuing delay, confusion, and behind-the-scenes tactics can be discouraging to even the most dedicated. Given the determination of Ed Meese and his White House aides to stack my department and my equally fervent resolve to prevent this, it is not difficult to fathom the reasons for the inordinate delays in consummating subcabinet appointments in ED.

I lived through this experience for most of 1981. Indeed, it was late November before we started to see success in getting our presidentially appointed people confirmed by the Senate and functioning in their leadership responsibilities.

How could I fight back? We reviewed our options many times. We knew the ultimate power rested with the President, and Ed Meese and his staff had many opportunities to tell Ronald Reagan how recalictrant I was in responding to their proposals of names to fill their key positions. Meese could walk into his office at will, while my opportunities were very limited.

There was the Office of Cabinet Affairs, directed by Craig Fuller, who was the in-house representative of cabinet officers' concerns and responsible for facilitating communication between the cabinet and the White House. But he was new to government and certainly subordinate to Meese and Baker. Craig eventually became a persuasive and respected senior White House officer, but it took several months for him to establish effective working relationships and authority. So I was on my own during the first months of 1981.

In May 1981, as I pursued my own low-key investigation to get at the roots of my trouble in the White House personnel shop, I learned that there were several feuds brewing. The people in the National Security Office were having a stressful time with Al Haig, the secretary of state. Al and Defense Secretary Cap Weinberger had had a few difficult innings. And Jeane Kirkpatrick, our United Nations ambassador, was having Rodney Dangerfield "I don't get no respect" trouble with the Department of State.

But the big-time trouble was the early splitting of the White House staff into the Jim Baker and Ed Meese camps. Jim Baker worked very closely with Richard Darman. Darman, a former HEW staffer during the Nixon-Ford years, was Baker's right-hand man; he later became deputy treasury secretary during Reagan's second term. Ed Meese had a faithful lieutenant in the person of Kenneth Cribb. Cribb, a movement conservative from South Carolina, steadily attained more power in the White House as Meese assigned him added responsibilities. Cribb and Darman quickly established a relationship of deep-seated mutual distrust, and this added fuel to the feud between Baker and Meese. Ken was a very short, dynamic knight of the right, and his alert eyes and ears picked up all the information that might be in the atmosphere, on peoples' lips, or in a wastebasket.

Because of his close friendship with Penn James, Meese and his camp had far more clout with the White House Personnel Office than did Baker. My investigation revealed that there were several cabinet departments in which the movement people especially wanted to place keepers of the faith, both because it was a loss of face not to have some of their own there and for inside dope. They wanted to be able to monitor deliberations about proposed actions and have early warning of what might be brewing in suspect agencies. ED was high on that list of departments.

However, there was one appointment that seemed to me to have enough high-level White House support to merit approval. David Stockman, director of the Office of Management and Budget, suggested that the very competent Chester Finn be appointed deputy undersecretary for planning and budget in ED. Finn had served in the Nixon White House. I had known him from my Nixon-Ford years, and I knew that I could work with him. Given Stockman's support, I was hopeful that he would be the first one to break the logjam. But despite this endorsement, Finn was promptly rejected by White House Personnel because he was currently serving on the staff of Democratic Senator Pat Moynihan. (Stockman and Finn had both been close to Moynihan during their Harvard days.) That was enough to do him in. I failed to win clearance for Finn.

Numerous other attempts at appointment consensus also failed. We simply could not agree on high-level people who required presidential appointment. A few lower-level appointees trickled through the tight procedure, but we made little progress on the major positions. I knew that with time the pressure outside as well as within Washington would build for a solution, and I had to survive until this heat was felt at the White House.

Typical of the Washington scene, one of the lesser topics of gossip around the cocktail circuit centered on how various cabinet members were getting along with White House staff. I was usually the one described as dwelling in disasterville.

In April 1981 I began to get inquiries from the press about my appointments to subcabinet positions. "How many have been cleared by White House personnel and sent on to the president?" The questioners knew the answer. I simply responded that I did not discuss personnel matters. But there was no doubt in their minds that I was being stonewalled at the White House personnel level.

The inquiries continued. Specific instances, including names of rejected candidates, were mentioned. This told me that White House staff members with access to the information were leaking these particulars to the press. Part of the strategy of Washington power politics is to hit your opponents with press leaks. A few facts are sprinkled in among outlandish or false conclusions. There are hundreds of journalists constantly circulating in Washington, so this technique can place a target, whether a cabinet officer, agency head, or other official, on the defensive. As the rumors grow the perception of problems or, in this case, of weakness and ineptness also expands dramatically.

It was clear there was a deliberate movement under way to destroy my credibility, and I had to counter it quickly and aggressively. Such political power base as I had was being drained. I had to get some appointments consummated or take some other action that would display strength, leadership, and decisiveness.

I needed an attention-getting issue unrelated to the senior staff stonewall. What could it be? I knew it had to be something of significance and also a move that would appeal to the conservative camp. I needed to win some grudging approval from at least the responsible conservatives who were close to the president and important to his power base. The radical right would never give me anything but trouble. I had no illusions about that.

One evening, churning this issue over and over in my mind, I came upon just the right move. My predecessor, Shirley Hufstedler, had sent up to the Hill some regulations concerning the bilingual education act. These rules were dead wrong. I was supportive of bilingual education, but these regulations prescribed a single method of teaching. In the way they were written, neither of the other two popular and effective approaches to teaching limited-English-proficient children could be used. The federal government was way off base in dictating teaching methodology to the teachers of America. I had known that I would eventually amend those rules, but I had planned to wait until we had settled in a bit more.

I decided, in that moment of illumination, to withdraw the regulations immediately and have Ted Sky, acting general counsel of the department, and his staff rewrite the entire package. There had been much nationwide discussion and strong criticism of the Hufstedler action. It would help my situation to move the timetable up.

Many conservatives hated bilingual education. Most of them hated it for the wrong reasons. They felt it would lead to disunity, strife, and even a movement, in areas of heavy Hispanic population, toward secession from the Union. I knew this was nonsense, but this far-out view had had widespread expression in some elements of the conservative press.

Rather than send amendments to the Hufstedler rules up to the Hill, I would sign an order to withdraw the entire package. Then we would start over, after holding hearings and learning more from the educational community.

The next day I began to set the stage for my action. I talked in confidence with Ted Sky. Ted was a very able career-executive service-level officer. I had known him for years in the old HEW. He was also a man of great ability, trustworthiness, and impeccable character. We discussed the bilingual regulations, and after I explained my concerns, he agreed that it might be best to start over in the legal drafting.

I then made a few quiet contacts to be certain the press would be ready and receptive. This took two or three more days.

After these preparations, I called a press conference in the Horace Mann Center at the Department of Education. I issued a press statement and a fact sheet on bilingual education. I attacked the concept of government prescription of teaching methods.

"If we start with bilingual education, where will it stop?" I asked. "We must stop this before we establish a precedent that will give federal bureaucrats power over the curriculum of all the schools across the nation."

This action hit the evening network television news. The next morning the newspapers nationwide carried the story of my attack on bilingual education rules.

My telephone began to ring. School administrators, teachers, and school board leaders congratulated me. It turned out to be the right move, and the timing could not have been better.

The following Tuesday, as I walked into the cabinet room at the White House, I received accolades from many of my colleagues. Even Ed Meese and Interior Secretary James Watt nodded their approval.

This simple action, which was ultimately going to be necessary anyway, helped my political position during those initial months when I was in a crisis period in my tenure in the cabinet. I had gained a much-needed respite from my adversaries. They did not stop, of course; the pressure simply eased for a short time. But the embattled education secretary had at least taken one decisive action. It was an attention getter that gave the public something else to think about.

Like the well-known law of physics that states that every action has an equal and opposite reaction, my action on the bilingual education rules led to a reaction. Hispanic leaders from across the nation sounded an alarm. I heard from Hispanic members of Congress. The leaders of the National Association for Bilingual Education called at my office. The department's Office of Bilingual Education and Minority Language Affairs (OBEMLA) was swamped with calls.

I had known there would be some misinterpretation of my objective in proposing new rules, misconstruing my attitude toward bilingual education. But the reaction was even stronger than I anticipated. The effects of my action soon spilled over into the Oval Office. Hispanics nationwide were calling the president. They feared that this was a harbinger of moves by the Reagan administration that would be inimical to their future well-being. This was never my intent. I had long felt that the Hispanic people in our country had been treated shabbily. Our education system had not met their needs. They had a proud heritage, and I earnestly wanted to be their friend. But these rules would not serve their needs either. They had to go.

Because people in political life must worry about perception and image, many actions that would draw little attention in a normal environment outside Washington are magnified many times in the nation's capital. Senators and representatives from areas with many Hispanics found in my withdrawal of the bilingual education rules an opportunity to champion the Hispanic cause. They wrote letters that were addressed to me or to the President, but they were really drafted with their constituents in mind.

Ronald Reagan had drawn strong support from Hispanics in his 1980 campaign. He needed to respond to the nationwide concern he was hearing from some of his campaign contributors and friends. He therefore held a meeting for national Hispanic leaders in the East Wing of the White House. There was a luncheon in the first-floor dining room and a discussion in the family theater. I was invited to host a table at the luncheon and to respond to questions in the discussion session. Vice President Bush also hosted a table and shared in the discussion. Elizabeth Dole, assistant to the president and wife of Senator Robert Dole, helped us in this fence-mending operation as well. Mrs. Dole is a very bright, skilled, and gracious administrator, and her capabilities were most welcome on this occasion. (She later became U.S. secretary of transportation, with her talents more fully recognized by advancement to cabinet rank. A Harvard Law School graduate with an undergraduate degree from Duke University, this North Carolinian is destined for a larger role in the nation's leadership structure.)

The White House meeting with Hispanic leaders provided an opportunity for me to display both my knowledge of the issues in bilingual education and some capacity for diplomacy before the president. It was important to establish my personal credibility, and I worked hard to be prepared. This was a first opportunity to give the president some political support, and I did not waste it. We discussed the English as a Second Language (ESL) method that was used in many schools that served Hispanic students. Knowing that the ESL approach was not permitted under the rules that I had withdrawn, I was able to persuade listeners of the sense behind the action we had taken. I also asked the leaders of several Hispanic organizations to work with my staff to draft new regulations. It was an effective session, and it defused the tension and clarified our objectives.

But the bilingual issue, however effective, helped me only temporarily. Though I was now in the position of having gained a small amount of added prestige, the deadlock on appointments had to be resolved and the subcabinet offices filled as quickly as possible.

So in July, I enlisted the help of Craig Fuller, White House director of cabinet affairs, to get some momentum.

Though he reported to Ed Meese, he also worked closely with Jim Baker, White House chief of staff. By now he had increased his ability to influence decisions, and I sensed that his power of persuasion had expanded to a point where he would be helpful.

Although little was spelled out about my predicament, Craig understood the whole plot. I knew he could plead my case with Meese, warning him and others that press attention to the staffing problems at ED was getting more intense each day and that something had to be done to resolve them.

Craig Fuller talked to Penn James several times about the need to get ED's senior staff on board. He heard White House concerns about what it felt was my rigidity about staffing. He suggested to me that it might be time for a compromise. I agreed.

There were other tactics that I could have tried, such as enlisting the support of the array of education organizations and associations that have headquarters in Washington. This large and influential education lobby was strongly interested in who was controlling the Department of Education, and they had begun to query their friends in Congress about what was going on. The lobby includes some very politically powerful college and university presidents as well as school superintendents, school board leaders, and others.

Congressional friends of ED who were the recipients of their phone calls, telegrams, and letters, began to pressure me. But it was a course I elected not to take; this was an internal administration struggle, and I wanted to fight my own battles. Broken confidences and leaks were games for others to play.

Ready now to compromise as Craig Fuller had suggested, I agreed to accept a movement conservative to see whether my proposals might find a reciprocal acceptance, and I approved Daniel Oliver to be the general counsel for the Department of Education. Dan was a lawyer, though most recently he had served as senior editor of the conservative journal, *National Review.*

After he joined ED's senior staff, I had agreement on my candidate, Dr. Vincent Reed, former superintendent of schools for the District of Columbia, to serve as assistant secretary for elementary and secondary education. Vincent was a moderate Republican and a well-known educator in the nation's capital. I then accepted Edward Curran, a conservative, as the director of the National Institute of Education. At the time of Curran's appointment he was working in a senior-level position in the White House personnel office. I was very pleased when this was followed by approval for Dr. Thomas Melady, president of Sacred Heart University, to become our assistant secretary for higher education. Tom Melady, a close friend of George Bush, was a lifelong Republican and had been given high-level consideration for the position of secretary of education. He came from the academic community (which I knew made him suspect in the eyes of the movement people) and was extremely able.

The Oliver appointment broke the logjam, and we moved ahead on appointments. There was never a verbal or a written agreement on trading, but I knew I had to have experienced administrators who were thoroughly familiar with the education programs under their direction in the line positions. Whenever I agreed to an interview with one of the opposition's key candidates I would emphasize my need for specific educators, highly respected in academe, in these positions. Nonetheless I was apprehensive about the ideologues I had agreed to, for I realized I was bringing potential trouble into ED.

After these agreements were reached, of course, we had the inevitable delays of full field investigations by the FBI and the process of Senate confirmation, and this added weeks to the appointment process.

A big break for me was the successful negotiation to have William Clohan become the undersecretary of education. Bill had been working as counsel to the House Education and Labor Committee. He had also served on the transition team for ED, so he seemed to be trusted in the White House hierarchy.

I erroneously concluded that Dr. Gary Jones was in the inner circle of my critics because he had been active in the Reagan campaign following several years as a top official in the Republican think tank, the American Enterprise Institute. I accepted him with reluctance as deputy undersecretary, but I came to realize that he was a responsible conservative, and he proved to be a very able and loyal colleague.

Dr. Robert Worthington, former assistant commissioner for vocational education in the New Jersey Department of Education was approved as assistant secretary for adult and vocational education. Mrs. Jean Tufts, former president of the National School Boards Association, became assistant secretary for the Office of Special Education and Rehabilitation Services.

I had a special request from Chief of Staff Jim Baker that I try to place Robert Billings in a suitable position in ED. Bob, a Baptist minister, had been close to Jerry Falwell of the Moral Majority. I knew that the president had a special interest in a Billings placement, and though Baker was very careful not to mention the president, I realized that this was to be a high-level request. Indeed, when Billings came to ED the press displayed unusual interest in him and in his assignment. Newspapers kept probing to learn if I had offered Billings a position under duress. But I accepted Jim Baker's suggestion knowing that I was not under special pressure to do so. I placed Billings in charge of our regional offices, and he did a fine job for us. He turned out to be a loyal friend, who became the target of criticism from some former colleagues because of his loyalty to me.

At long last, the often painful struggle over presidential appointments was behind me. It had taken too long; there were some compromises I would rather not have made, and some that proved very happy ones; and I had succeeded in assembling a staff that was a balance between moderates and ideologues, making it possible for me to have credibility in the education community as well as to do my job.

It had been a rocky start, but I finally proved to some of my White House adversaries that I would not be intimidated or dominated. This was essential at the outset. I simply had to fight my way through this initial attack. I didn't win, but most importantly, I didn't lose either.

We had a standoff, and there was much more to come before I concluded four long and weary years working in an administration that wanted me to go home while I still felt I had some unfinished business in Washington.

CHAPTER 5

The Movement Conservatives and the Reagan Administration

||||||||||||||||||||||||||||||||||||||||||||||||||||||||||||||||||||||||||||||||||||||||||||||||||||||||||||||||||||||||||||||||||||||

Not long after the impasse over senior appointments in ED was broken, the people from the movement realized that they had allowed control of the federal financial assistance programs to schools and colleges to slip through their fingers. The secretary, undersecretary, and most of the assistant secretaries who controlled education program dollars were not movement conservatives. I had deliberately put experienced educators in charge of grants and daily contacts with the nationwide educational community. But the movement people could be found in ample number in high-level support-staff positions such as that of general counsel, in the budget and management offices, in educational research posts, and in regional office liaison, all posts in which they could monitor much that went on in the department and raise questions based on the facts they garnered.

Dan Oliver, general counsel; Edward Curran, director of NIE; Charles Heatherly, departmental executive secretary; Robert Billings, chief of our regional office liaison unit; Donald Seneese, assistant secretary for the Office of Educational Research and Evaluation; and several other movement people in lesser positions made up the roster of conservatives in ED when staffing was finally concluded. Some members of this group started holding weekly Wednesday luncheon meetings. I had my own infiltrator in their ranks, a high-ranking conservative in whom they had misplaced their trust. He was one of them, but he was also my friend.

From this source I learned that I would soon begin to feel the pressure of a carefully planned campaign to force me out of office. Failing that, the Wednesday luncheon participants planned to strangle the infant Department of Education through actions that attacked those presidentially appointed subcabinet members who worried them. They also planned to discredit the programs of financial assistance to students, schools, and colleges. Those who were on my senior staff fed information and copies of issue papers to their fellow true believers and supplied leaks to the press as part of their campaign.

The Wednesday group was well situated to execute its plans because its members were so well placed in influential positions in OMB, the Justice Department, and the West Wing that it was easy to keep the heat on me.

ED was, of course, not their only target. Other agencies were also victims, especially the Departments of Health and Human Services and State, where the knights of the hard right were unremittingly on Haig's tail. With the Californians on the senior White House staff and some of his department colleagues also after him, his position appeared even less tenable than mine.

My informer in the Wednesday group who briefed me about the plans to "get" certain people over at State proved to be right on the mark. Sure enough, there were leaked stories in the conservative press, and questions and accusations were leveled at them during hearings on the Hill before the Senate Foreign Relations Committee, where Senator Jesse Helms of North Carolina kept the heat on Haig.

The pressure on State didn't mean an easing of the squeeze on me. Through my source I soon learned that my undersecretary, Bill Clohan, was going to be the first of my senior staff to feel the sting. I didn't pay much attention to this report at first, but a successful strategy to discredit Bill soon convinced me that I was wrong. By March of 1982, White House-generated criticism of Clohan was in full bloom.

Bill was a young lawyer, a West Virginia Republican, and a graduate of the Air Force Academy. He was bright, personable, capable, and loyal. I liked him. We were working well together.

In a public meeting with the Council of Chief State School Officers, the organization comprising state commissioners of education and state superintendents of public instruction, Bill was interrogated about the president's commitment to tuition tax credits. We had the main elements of the president's proposal ready to release in a few days, but the details were being carefully guarded until the president made his announcement from the White House. In response to intense questioning, Bill loyally defended the administration's position. When the question as to the timing of action was raised, Bill responded that the program would be announced soon. That was all he said, but that was enough.

The exchange between the undersecretary and the chief state school officers was quoted in the press. Ed Meese directed Penn James to express the White House's dismay at what had appeared in the newspapers. Bill was accused of leaking a White House decision prematurely. I defended him vigorously. I knew that this matter was being distorted deliberately to trigger a reaction. In a day or two Penn James called to tell me they wanted Bill's resignation immediately. I protested that Bill had not given any details, that this was an abrupt decision, and that both Ed Meese and Penn were overreacting. It was not fair to Bill, and I was very pleased with his work. Penn reminded me that the undersecretary served at the pleasure of the president. In government we call this minute-to-minute tenure.

On May 2, 1982, Penn called again and insisted that he have Clohan's resignation; the decision was irrevocable. Defeated, I called Bill into my office and told him that he was fired. He promptly wrote out his resignation and handed it to me. My adversaries from the right had drawn first blood. It was painful, unfair, and frightening.

The West Virginia congressional delegation demanded an explanation for the firing. They called the White House. The response was that I had asked for Bill's resignation. They should call me. I refused to comment. The press tried to get a story from me, but I remained tight-lipped.

The education lobby took up the cause. House Republicans who had worked closely with Bill before he resigned to work for me demanded emphatically that I release an explanation. Was the action mine? Was it ordered by the White House? I stood fast in my refusal to comment.

Rumors started that I would be next, but the jubilation of my conservative critics intensified my resolve to hold on. Close friends in the education community called to urge me to hang tough. They feared the consequences of turning ED over to the extreme right wing. I simply told them that I knew I enjoyed the confidence of the President and that I would be around for a long time. I didn't believe it, but I said it anyway. Ed Meese could get me just as he had Bill, but I was not going to admit that to anyone.

It was important to stay because I had a commitment from the president that the initiative to draft the proposal to abolish ED would come from my office. I wanted to see this through and assure a continuing federal role for education as we placed the department in a newly structured agency with less-than-cabinet status. Somehow I had to learn how to work with the administration.

But how could I be a loyal team player and get my way? How could I persuade the president to recognize that there was a critical role for the federal government in education? How could I work from within the cabinet to represent the needs of American education? This wasn't going to be easy; the firing of Bill Clohan brought that home. I had a narrow line to tread. I needed time to build my political base. Right then I was as vulnerable as Bill Clohan, and there was no way I could carry out my plans from a position of weakness. I reasoned that I must bide my time—and hope I had it—let the administration mellow out, and get some rough edges knocked off. Then I could look for an opportunity to make my moves. This was a time for caution.

The ultraconservatives who had been placed in my department had ample opportunity to find horror stories if one looked at our operations from their perspective. We had women's educational equality act awards, school desegregation assistance grants, teacher center funding, and many other disbursements. Since the conservatives opposed all federal funding, they could simply sift through the awards and highlight those that were likely not to be made by a conservative administration.

Because many grants had been made on a multiyear basis prior to my taking office, and because appropriations bills mandated their continuation, legally we had to comply with all such awards. For example, we were specifically directed in the appropriations law to fund one program that was sponsored by the Reverend Jesse Jackson. This was known as the PUSH/EXCELL program to motivate minority students to improve their academic achievement. Assistant Secretary Vincent Reed had never been excited by the results of this initiative. Since he was a very distinguished black educator with extensive experience working with inner-city minority children, I respected his views. But both of us soon learned that we had to fund Jackson's project despite our misgivings about its effectiveness. At first, we withheld the release of the PUSH/EXCELL funds, but the pressure to reinstitute them quickly escalated. Audits by ED staff determined that despite sloppy bookkeeping, the funds had been spent according to law.

General Counsel Dan Oliver was opposed to making this award. But the career lawyers in ED, whom I had known from previous years, were advising me privately that I could become personally liable for willful failure to comply with the law. However, these career people worked under Oliver's direction so they were naturally circumspect in giving advice publicly that was contrary to that offered by their boss.

Dan Oliver used this situation to put me on the hot seat, but I believe that he knew that I had to approve the grant despite the questionable results of previous years of funding.

When Dr. Reed and I finally decided we had to release the funds as directed by the appropriations law, the reaction was immediate. The conservative press gave the action ample exposure. The talebearers in ED kept midlevel White House people on the Meese staff informed of all the reasons they could garner that implied the decision was the result of my left-leaning tendencies.

Not long after this, *Conservative Digest* came out with an issue that featured me on the cover as a gasoline station attendant filling up trucks bearing labels such as NEA and PUSH/EXCELL and buses that were being used to attain racial balance in schools.

There were a multitude of problems spread across ED that had to be solved, and until we corrected them I was vulnerable to attacks like these from my adversaries. In addition to the quality of the PUSH/EX-CELL program and its funding mandate, we had college-student-loan defaults, civil rights enforcement issues on the college level in several states, and trouble brewing in our educational research program.

Edward Curran, director of the National Institute of Education, found numerous programs in NIE to criticize. Since he was a member of the movement, he discussed many ills in the research program inherited from the Carter days with his fellow conservatives. I supported him in actions he took to correct funding of research projects with little promise, but I was adamant about sustaining others.

The NIE has a network of education laboratories and research centers spread across the nation. These units were working with state and local schools to implement research findings that showed particular promise to enhance teaching and learning. Some very respectable projects were under way, and I insisted that these be continued. For example, our past years of research had provided valuable insights into the teaching of reading. The evidence gathered about the value of teaching phonics convinced educators to change teaching practice. Stronger phonics programs were now being placed in the most popular reading series. Other NIE-funded studies proved that the so-called modern mathematics programs used extensively in many schools had serious deficiencies, again an impetus for important changes.

Laboratories and research centers had also done valuable work on the use of computers in the schools. Given the increasing interest and continuing advances in computer technology and the importance of this field, this work merited our support. Indeed, I prevailed on David Stockman to increase our appropriations in this area.

When I interviewed Ed Curran before I endorsed his appointment, I had discussed the federal role in education research. The institute's budget was small and its contacts with schools and colleges minimal compared to the billions of dollars and the huge impact of the offices of the assistant secretary for higher education and the assistant secretary for elementary and secondary education. Moreover, it had never realized its potential nor been given credit for what it did achieve; its public relations and congressional support left much to be desired. But given Curran's degrees from Yale and Duke, and a respectable reputation as headmaster of an outstanding private school, I had felt he would be a good bet to succeed as the director of NIE. I knew from our discussion that he would press hard on the back-to-basics theme, but that was fine; I favored this too.

Curran proposed Robert Sweet, a New Hampshire book salesman and former teacher, as his deputy director (a presidentially appointed job but not one requiring Senate approval). Sweet was also a movement conservative, but I believed that Curran was entitled to his choice for deputy and acceded. (The same logic governed my okaying Dan Oliver's choice of Joseph Beard, a North Carolina conservative, as his deputy general counsel; he had the right to choose the person who would serve directly under him.)

But before very long, I discovered that my optimism about Curran's role at NIE was unwarranted. He decided that he was the head of an organization that was wasting money, doing no good, and should be abolished. Curran knew that under the federal act that created the Department of Education, only the secretary had the authority to change or abolish certain units within it, and NIE was one of these; but I was determined to give the institute the chance to prove its worth. Curran knew that too.

He also knew, of course, that Ed Meese, who was fast becoming the most powerful man in the government next to the president, wanted to abolish NIE, and that I had debated its future with Meese. (Though NIE was a creation of the Nixon administration, there was a misconception at the White House that it was yet one more product of the liberal Democrats who held power during the Carter years.) Here was Ed Curran's chance to make a bold move and win plaudits and hero status with the movement chiefs.

When he decided that NIE should be abolished, he did not choose to discuss it with me. He wrote directly to the president, and he "forgot" to send me a copy. His letter said his institute was wasting money and doing no good and that the federal government had no role in education research. It ended with a plea that NIE be abolished.

The letter was a very clever piece of strategy. The word *abolish* was the most popular verb associated with ED. Since it appeared that I was not moving decisively to abolish the entire department, my director of NIE would nudge me along the way by asking the President to do what he knew I would not do.

I was furious, of course, when Dick Darman, deputy to Chief of Staff Jim Baker, referred the letter to me for review and comment. True to Washington's tradition, the letter was also leaked to the press. The cynics who specialize in cabinet watching started speculating what I would do.

I decided Curran thought that he could make his move and I would have to go along with it or lose my job. It did not take me long to decide on my course of action, though I could not be certain of the outcome. The challenge to my authority had to be met firmly, without equivocation. Since the Curran letter was transmitted to me without a request for my recommendation to the president, I gave Darman a quick, direct response: I was wholly opposed to the recommendation, and I wanted Curran fired.

Curran was presidentially appointed, so such an action had to be taken at the White House. This would be a test for the president and his senior staff. It would be especially hard for Ed Meese to accede to the dismissal of a loyal conservative.

Mary Jean Letendre, a special assistant in my office who had had years of experience in Washington (as had her husband, who had served in the Nixon White House), confirmed this. "Not only is this matter difficult for you—it puts the White House in a dilemma," she told me.

Personnel Chief Penn James called to ask if I was convinced this was the best course of action. Some advisors in the department and one good friend over at the White House suggested it might be more prudent to reprimand Curran and then keep him. I was not about to do that. In the Washington game of chicken you don't blink. This was likely to be only the first of such confrontations.

My executive assistant and chief of staff, Elam Hertzler, sized the matter up when he said: "You can't let Ed get away with this trick. From my phone calls I can tell you that the education community is watching this one to see what you'll do."

"I don't have any choice but to demand Curran's resignation," I told him and Mary Jean. "In fact, I did that yesterday. They want me to reconsider, however."

"Don't do it. Stick to your guns," Hertzler advised.

"What if they refuse?" Sharon Schonhaut asked. Sharon was the other professional staff member who served in the immediate office of the secretary. Having grown up in Brooklyn, Sharon knew that confrontation had to be weighed carefully in anticipation of the consequences that might follow.

"I will go directly to the president. I'll explain the situation in detail. Then I'll resign if he doesn't support me. But that should never go out of this room. I've learned that you never threaten to resign. You either go or you stay."

Sharon was startled. "You mean you'd quit your cabinet job just over this?"

"There is no way that Curran can stay on as director of NIE after it's widely known that he wrote directly to the president and told him the mission of NIE was unnecessary," I told her.

That afternoon I received a phone call from Craig Fuller of the Office of Cabinet Affairs. "Ted, if you need to see the president, just let me know," Craig offered.

He himself could not get into the escalating conflict. He never let himself become embroiled in the many fights among members of the top echelon of the Reagan administration. But I recognized that this offer was an expression of sympathy.

"I don't think that this matter needs to get into the Oval Office. At least, not just yet," I said.

I knew that Jim Baker would understand why I was playing hardball. I also knew that Pennington James understood the situation. He had a broad understanding of government and procedures, and he recognized that a cabinet officer could not tolerate insubordination. Indeed, I was counting on Penn James's common sense to prevail. He was a close friend of Meese, and the decision would be made there unless circumstances forced it up into the Oval Office. My strategy was to make it plain that that's where it would end up if the decision went against me.

Ed Meese was the point of concern. I felt I was in fairly good standing in all places but there.

Meese would want to do more violence to the federal role in education than I could tolerate. If he could get me out just as he had fired Bill Clohan as undersecretary, it would avoid pain for him later. It would also draw applause from the movement people.

To my relief and great pleasure, the decision to fire Ed Curran, or at least to transfer him out of ED to another position, came shortly after my conversation with Craig Fuller. Jim Baker let me know that I would receive full support from the White House. This meant that the

Baker side had won, and Meese was not going to see the matter go to the president.

Ed Curran then came to my office to present me with a copy of the letter and to apologize profusely for his oversight in not sending it to me earlier. (Even then, I failed to hear him say that the letter should have gone through me to the President.) He wanted to keep his job. He assured me that he could perform his duties as the NIE chief with great distinction despite the publicity surrounding his letter. I knew better, and my decision was firm.

Curran was subsequently appointed to serve as deputy director of the Peace Corps. Months later he was nominated by the president to succeed Dr. William Bennett as director of the National Endowment for the Humanities. The sorry chapter he had written in the history of NIE thus came before the Senate committee. His nomination was rejected by the Senate in one of those rare occasions when a presidential nominee does not win approval.

Following the Curran episode I began to feel the full heat of the movement's anger. They continued to receive inside information on virtually everything that went on in ED, and my often unhappy tenure became even more so. After the removal of Curran, I had to propose an new name for NIE director, but in the interim I named Bob Sweet to serve as acting director. (I had no choice, since the deputy director was the only other presidentially appointed official at NIE.) But Sweet used this opportunity to launch his own campaign to be appointed permanently. I received phone calls, letters from senators, and even assurances that the appointment of Sweet would heal all my wounds with the far right.

I knew that Bob was not the right person to head up NIE because he lacked strong credentials in educational research. But my choice also had to have a long history of support for Reagan, if he or she was to win White House approval.

Fortunately I found just the right person. He was Hispanic. He had a record of Reagan support going back to the Ford-Reagan fight for the nomination in 1976. Dr. Manuel Justiz, professor of education at the University of New Mexico, was my choice for this hot spot.

The administration was being criticized for its failure to place minority candidates in top positions. I had heard an admonition about this in a recent cabinet meeting. We were particularly deficient in senior-level Hispanic appointees. The president had been popular with Hispanics in the 1980 election, but we needed to do some fence-mending.

Justiz was a Cuban refugee and a committed Republican. He lived in the Southwest, where he had strong rapport with Mexican Americans.

He was young and attractive. He had the support of the New Mexico congressional delegation, including Senator Pete Domenici, chair of the Senate Budget Committee.

I sent Dr. Justiz's name over to the White House, and there were immediate phone calls from the Baker faction praising the choice as a master stroke. The Meese contingent would have trouble opposing such a well-qualified Republican candidate.

The nomination was quickly approved at the White House, and his name was sent up to the Senate for confirmation. But to my surprise, this ideal choice generated opposition in the Senate. The chief source was from Bob Sweet's home state of New Hampshire. His senator, Humphrey, put an immediate hold on the Justiz nomination, and his name languished in the Senate instead of whizzing through under the sponsorship of Pete Domenici and with the support of the chairman of the Senate Labor and Human Resources Committee, my good friend and fellow Utahan, Orrin Hatch.

Movement conservatives opposed Justiz, and that made it difficult for Hatch. Since Sweet was one of their own and since Justiz was a moderate Republican, it was in their interest to defeat the nomination. They were the source of all kinds of rumors about Justiz. Perception in Washington is almost as potent as reality. Justiz was not being hurt by any valid accusations; he was simply getting the fallout from the rumor mill. Once the mill starts turning, it feeds on its own momentum, no matter how unwarranted the allegations are. Facts are never relevant in struggles like this.

Happily, there was no upsurge of opposition despite the rumors, and opposition to the nomination subsided in a few days. The Justiz nomination was moved out of committee and approved on the Senate floor. I breathed a sign of relief. The NIE-Curran episode was over. It was time to turn my efforts to more productive endeavors.

But my belief that I had seen the last of my NIE troubles was wrong. After Justiz was sworn in he came to me to say that he could not work with Robert Sweet as deputy director. I briefed him on the sensitive matters related to Curran's departure; this was not the time to discharge another problem conservative. We had them all over the place, and he would have to endure his fair share of the problems they created.

Justiz promised to do his best to coexist but a few days later he was back in my office with horror tales of Sweet and his disruptive disciples. They refused to take direction from him, and he could not run the place under such conditions.

He was right, but the fact remained that we had had enough uproar for a while, and I was very reluctant to act. Since Sweet, too, was presidentially appointed, I would have to go through the White House again. I looked around for an alternative job for Sweet, but nothing seemed to fit. I was weary of the mess, but it stayed with me like the plague.

And the plague was destined to spread.

At this point, a presidentially appointed council entered the plot. When NIE was created, hopes were strong that we could do some significant research on teaching and learning in the United States. There is much to discover about how children learn, how they are motivated, and what presentations of subject matter lead to optimal results. In order to set the priorities for a research agenda and to help guide the policies of the institute, a National Council on Educational Research (NCER) was formed. The legislation that the Nixon administration sponsored through Congress mandated that the members of this council be appointed by the president. The idea was to create a very prestigious body to set the policy for research priorities of the Institute.

When the NCER members' names came up for reappointment by the new administration, it was decided that President Reagan should discharge all those who had been appointed back in the Carter and Ford eras without waiting for their terms of office to expire. There were a few grumblings, but the appointees left without too much fuss.

A panel of new NCER members went up to the Hill for Senate confirmation without much fanfare and were routinely approved. The new chairman of the council was George Roche, president of Hillsdale College in Michigan. George was a staunch conservative, a bright man, and a person who took a dim view of the past research agenda of NIE. I shared many of his concerns.

When I removed Curran and selected Justiz as the new director, word reached me that Chairman Roche was upset with my actions, as was the department's general counsel, Daniel Oliver. What happened when these two got together to fix things in NIE would provide a fine plot for a comic opera. Observers on the Washington scene—especially ED watchers at the *Washington Post*—found the next turn of events uproariously funny. I should have laughed too, but I was too angry to do anything but alternately scream and smolder.

NCER had authority to employ an executive director and other staff members. Throughout the history of NIE, the executive director of NCER had served on the NIE director's staff, and NIE people provided NCER with clerical and staff assistance. Funds were saved with this arrangement, and the director was kept in a close working relationship with the council. Through the Nixon-Ford-Carter years the arrangement worked well.

Dan Oliver wrote a general counsel opinion for George Roche defining the powers of NCER. Like Curran with his letter to the President, he "forgot" to send me a copy. The opinion gave NCER a separate staff that was independent of the director of NIE. By carefully scrutinizing the law and torturing it a bit, Dan was also able to conclude that NCER was the chief policy-making body for all aspects of NIE. This would give NIE a degree of independence from the secretary of education.

The Oliver opinion was written with care, and I had no knowledge that the plot was under way until the pie was baked and put before me. To make it even more unsavory, the council voted to appoint Robert Sweet to serve as its executive director. This action was taken by vote of the council at one of its regularly scheduled meetings. Directions then flowed from Chairman Roche to Sweet and Justiz. The result was to place Justiz, NIE's director, in a position subordinate to the council and to put Sweet in a position where he could act on behalf of the council in giving Justiz his marching orders. This may appear to be a proper action for the council to take, but it ignores the provisions of law that created ED and established the authority of the secretary of education. All presidentially appointed officers reported to me. I was not going to tolerate NIE reporting separately to a council outside my line of authority.

I couldn't believe my eyes as I read the Oliver opinion. Sweet, Roche, and Oliver had acted with finesse in turning the tables on the cabinet officer who had removed their good friend, Curran, and bypassed Sweet for the director's post.

The council met again soon after Sweet's appointment. He presented a series of resolutions that in effect put him in control of NIE, with a staff and a council budget of $834,000 at his disposal. This action was followed by a series of memos from Sweet to Justiz demanding information and responses that, if followed, would undercut the director's authority.

I had an angry confrontation with Dan Oliver over his opinion. He innocently denied doing anything but objectively reading the statute and interpreting it to the chairman of NCER. I stormed over to the White House to demand that those responsible for the Roche appointment force him to remove Sweet from his new post.

This effort yielded quick results. Sweet was offered a job in the White House. I was told that the matter had been sent to the president, and he had ordered an end to the silly game that had gone on for an incredible ten months. I never did learn the details of how the decision came about, but at long last I had both Ed Curran and Bob Sweet out of the department.

The *Washington Post* summed up the bureaucratic squabble in a story that ran under the headline: ''Education Department Aide is Tackled on End Run.'' The story was illustrated with a photograph of my scowling countenance before a microphone where I was dancing and sparring my way through a press conference without saying anything that would embarrass the President.

Relations were so strained between Oliver and me after this episode that I had to ask for his removal as well. Since Oliver was working at a higher level in ED than Sweet and Curran, it took some time to find him a new job. He was eventually appointed general counsel to the U.S. Department of Agriculture.

I proposed the appointment of Maureen Corcoran, a talented young lawyer from San Francisco, to succeed Oliver. Her Republican credentials were in order, and we needed more women in high positions in the Reagan administration. She turned out to be a very wise choice. Her nomination was readily accepted, and the president invited her to the Oval Office for her swearing-in ceremony.

Soon after Dan Oliver left ED his deputy, Joe Beard, moved over to the U.S. Department of Justice. I hadn't asked him to leave, but I assumed that he felt the new general counsel would want to select another deputy. Joe had written a memo on the education of handicapped children that was leaked to the press. It caused us some embarrassment, and I was constantly hassled about it when I testified on the Hill. We were happy to see Joe Beard make his move to Justice, for it gave us a chance to have an entire new team at both NIE and the Office of General Counsel.

It was an unseemly fight that led to the departure of four top-level members of the movement from ED. But it was crucial that I come across as a man who knew what he was doing and who was in control of his department. Not only my future but the future of a federal presence and significant role were at stake. At all costs I had to preserve that role. The longer I survived, the harder it would be for my opposition to accomplish its ends.

But as I knew from keeping in close touch with what was going on at the White House, that opposition was not only formidable, it required a wary and assessing eye on who was who in the power game being played by White House senior officials. Like Washington's political pros, the press, and the interested public, I was fascinated by the tripartite structure the president had put in place for his own staff. Jim Baker as chief of staff, Ed Meese as counselor to the president, and Mike Deaver as deputy chief of staff each had his own staff and each reported directly to the president—and each pressed for special access and authority.

There was a similar three-headed foreign policy–national security structure, comprising Secretary of State Al Haig, National Security Adviser Richard Allen, and Secretary of Defense Cap Weinberger mixing it up over who was in charge of what and also vying for presidential support. As I noted earlier, Al Haig became the first target of this struggle. A crucial issue in our early cabinet meetings was the conflict between foreign policy and the nation's economy, because the repercussions of Jimmy Carter's embargo on shipments of grain to the Soviets after the Afghanistan invasion had left our farmers without a major market for their huge grain surpluses. Haig wanted the administration to assume a tough, unyielding posture from the start; he was against concessions to the Soviets this early in our tenure. John Block, the secretary of agriculture, felt we were only hurting ourselves by continuing the embargo and pressed for a resumption of grain sales. Ultimately Haig had to capitulate—the first of a series of reversals that eventually forced his departure.

These conflicts played out by the foreign policy and senior White House staff trios were instructive (and sometimes daunting), given my uneasy position and uncertain status. I also thought them inevitable and I was surprised by the president's organizational decisions. In my years of managing the affairs of large and complex education organizations, I had learned that responsibilities had to be clearly fixed, with explicitly defined lines of authority and no overlap. Any ambiguity about authority or responsibility leads to disaster. I marveled that the president had not learned this lesson while governor of California. Eventually he ran into disaster from the ambiguity of authority in his national security apparatus—but it took six years when I thought it would happen in six months.

By watching the interaction between Richard Allen, and Al Haig, I was able to learn more about White House internal politics and the power equation. Allen, although respectably competent, was not a strong figure initially. Ever since the Henry Kissinger days, the occupant of this office had contended for power with the secretary of state. When Allen's positions on issues became dominant, it provided me with useful clues for the conduct of my duties. Being a relative lightweight in the cabinet, in what was obviously the most uncertain position of all, I had to be very circumspect. By watching what went on among the big players, I learned over time how to play my hand.

All intramural conflicts were suspended briefly in March of 1981 when news came that the president had been shot while leaving the Washington Hilton Hotel and was rushed to George Washington University Hospital for surgery. Vice President Bush was in Texas, but there was a specific procedure in place for emergencies. In the absence of both the president and vice president, the senior government official is the secretary of state. With the press urgently pressing for information, Al Haig responded in the White House pressroom and got himself into more hot water.

Haig and Weinberger had disagreed as to which of them should respond to the press, and when Al went to the pressroom, he appeared to be quite nervous and unsure of his role. This came across in his performance before the television cameras.

This pressroom behavior unquestionably hurt his image. But the manner in which the White House handled the situation told the rest of us a good deal about how a cabinet member in trouble could be left to bleed a little if he was not perceived to be a good team player. Haig insisted on being the one to speak for the administration, and he went before the press corps without the full support of the White House staff. His seniority in rank entitled him to do this, but the action was costly.

The vice president, acting during the illness of the president, must carry out his duties in a manner that does not display timidity and uncertainty on the one hand or eagerness on the other. The time of the president's convalescence was a very delicate period for George Bush, and he handled it admirably. He was a perfect vice president. In cabinet meetings he presided with dignity and poise. No hint of taking over the role of "Mr. President" came across the cabinet table.

During the period of the president's stay in the hospital, I checked carefully to learn about access to his bedside. This demonstrated the considerable strength of Jim Baker. It was instructive to see him grow in power and influence and to compare his technique with those of Al Haig and Richard Allen. Here was a brilliant man who had come to Washington best known as the campaign manager for George Bush in the early days of the 1980 campaign for the Republican presidential nomination. Now he was functioning as the president's chief of staff. He had to earn this respect and confidence in a somewhat hostile environment. Jim was clearly destined to be a winner in the Reagan administration.

The president soon was back on his feet. We were all amazed at how rapidly he recovered from his major surgery, displaying great vitality and even greater zest for his job.

With Ronald Reagan in good health again, the attention of the administration turned to matters of taxes, money, and the economy. I would soon learn my first lessons in supply-side economics.

CHAPTER 6

Supply-Side Medicine for the Economy

|||||||||||||||||||||||||||||||||||||||||||||||||||||||||||||||||||||||||||||||||||||||||||||||||||||||||||||||||||||||||||||||||||||||||||||||

The president's economic recovery program was now the top priority. We had a stagnant economy in the midst of high inflation, which led to the coining of a new term, *stagflation*. David Stockman was in his element; if he had relished wielding a budgetary ax before, it was nothing compared to his dominating role now.

The key to the entire economic agenda was a big tax cut. This was mandated by the passage of the Kemp-Roth bill, which the Reagan administration pushed through after extensive lobbying, jockeying, and stroking of conservative Democrats in the House. The tax cut was to be accompanied by enormous reductions in federal spending, a process facilitated by a second act, the Graham-Latta bill, which used Congress's budget machinery to reduce numerous expenditure levels in one fell swoop.

All I could do was play a damage control game at ED. My power base was too feeble to do much else. I resolved to bide my time. I also started to think about what I could do to enhance my image. This would require something quite dramatic. I needed an attention getter of some sort. I did not like my role as a puppy with its tail between its legs watching the big pooches take all the action.

I knew I had to accept the Stockman cuts. They were even more formidable than I expected. He intended to reduce the federal role in education to rubble, take away crucial aid to needy college students, and slash financial assistance that supplemented the education of the disadvantaged and the poor.

Moreover, I was going to have to defend these indefensible cuts on the Hill. I dreaded the scenes when it came time for appropriation hearings in the House and the Senate. My colleagues in education knew that I knew better. I could read the scorn on their faces. Here was a contemptible little white-haired man acceding to the betrayal of the nation's schools and colleges. For what? To them, my only motive would be to save my own position with the Reagan crowd.

In the interim I took a hard look at some ineffective federal education programs that should indeed be cut, and at the absurd number of separate aid programs to schools and colleges—120 of them—with a huge array of rules and regulations that explained the law, defined the intent of Congress, and told potential recipients how to qualify for funds. And that gave me an idea. . . .

During my years in the Nixon-Ford administration I had proposed that we consolidate many of these grants under a single law. We would then allocate the funds to schools in one lump sum and give local school boards broad discretion in the use of the money.

Richard Nixon was high on the concept of revenue sharing. The proposal became identified as "special revenue sharing for education," and we pushed hard in the old HEW for the legislation. Elliot Richardson was the secretary at the time, and he won White House approval for it. But when it came to Congress we hit a stone wall.

Now that Reagan had started his push for less government, less regulation, and a reduction in federal spending, I decided the time was ripe for this idea to get center stage again. Called a block grant, it received a warm reception from the White House, and from David Stockman at OMB. Block grants had been proposed for other federal programs and the application of the concept to education became part of our legislative program. Conservatives supported it as an interim measure until such time as they could reduce federal funding to zero. School administrators were generally supportive because they were weary of the intricacies of the numerous programs with which they had to contend.

But as we worked on the details of the proposal, we discovered that Stockman had placed forty-four unrelated federal education programs within the new block grant.

This included the huge Title I program of the Elementary and Secondary Education Act, passed back in 1965. This was a $3.5 billion program that provided assistance to schools in which there were concentrations of low-income and educationally disadvantaged students. The program reached thousands of schools all across the country. If Stockman's intent became law, this $3.5 billion could be diverted to any one of forty-three other, different purposes.

"For a bright guy, Stockman is certainly naive politically," I told my colleagues in ED as we discussed the outcome of one of my sessions over at OMB. "Would you believe it? He has the bilingual education program in that big pot. That means schools could take all the money for the disadvantaged and spend it on bilingual education."

"Are you going to go along with it?" asked a colleague.

"I think I have a way to disarm him," I responded.

The next day I was in the Old Executive Office Building facing Stockman in his office once more. My mission was to keep bilingual education out of the block grant.

I knew that my supply-side friend across the table wanted to cut spending. That was paramount. Any issue that might interfere with his ax would get his attention. "Dave, how would you like to increase the potential of having more federal money going to bilingual education by ten or twenty times?" I asked.

"You know my answer to that," he growled.

"That's what you're doing in the block grant," I countered.

"You're just touchy about your constituency," he said.

"Your block grant proposal has bilingual education, the three-and-a-half-billion-dollar Title One program, and forty-two other small federal aid programs all in the same pot. Under the draft legislation school districts may deploy the money for any purpose under the law. So, it is possible to increase by well over three billion the *potential* funding for bilingual education," I told him.

I knew that idea would catch his attention. I went on to remind him that his right-wing colleagues saw bilingual education as a guise used by Hispanics to perpetuate their language.

"I hadn't thought of that," he said. "Let's take it out and keep it separate at least for now."

I was smiling inside, but kept my face impassive. Stockman assured me he would make the change, and I left OMB knowing that I would not be caught in the crossfire of the conservative community and the Hispanic organizations on this matter. It was an explosive issue, and I didn't need any more battles right then.

The Stockman proposal to dump these program funds into the proposed new block was a prime example of mindless bureaucracy. The bilingual funds would have been spread evenly to all school districts on the basis of population and other factors totally unrelated to the number of students needing assistance because they could not speak or read English. School districts with no students in need of this special assistance would receive proportionately the same amount of the bilingual money as school systems with huge concentrations of non-English-speaking children.

This incident started to create in my mind an increased awareness of the need for a secretary of education. Until that point, I had reluctantly accepted the reality that came with my job: agreement to downgrade ED from cabinet to separate agency status. But this episode led me to question the wisdom of Reagan's idea. We *needed* a cabinet department and a secretary of education. Had education still been a subunit of HEW, I would never have been able to have direct access to David Stockman. The secretary of HEW would be the one to fight this battle, and the chances of him or her having expertise in this area would be very remote.

The phenomenon soon to wear the label of the Reagan revolution was born with the tax cuts, spending cuts, and deregulation and federal program simplification laws all enacted by Congress late in 1981. These actions brought the forces from the left, middle, and right down on my office. Senators and representatives converged on ED to see that the rules promulgated to implement the latest education laws were fashioned to their liking.

Congress enacted these and many other laws in a huge reconciliation act passed without the usual hearings. This unusual legislative maneuver made it possible for lawmakers to act without taking extensive testimony from interest groups or heads of agencies. Opportunity to lobby was not foreclosed, but it was drastically limited. Thus there was a vote on legislation that touched virtually the entire government without debate over the details. Lawmakers voted on a huge package, so they were able to plead innocence of details or express their devotion to the cause of cutting expenditures and reducing the burden on the government if a special group claimed it had been harmed.

But the absence of hearings was an exception, and my return to Washington brought me back to the familiar process of appearances before the House and Senate. Almost all my testimony was given before four committees: the Senate Labor and Human Resources Committee, the House Committee on Education and Labor (my most frequent appearances were before its education subcommittee), and the appropriations committees of the Senate and the House. I had appeared before many of these legislators during the Nixon-Ford era, but now that I was a cabinet official I realized the game had changed.

These sessions are contests for lawmakers as well as information-gathering situations. The committee chairs are appointed by the majority leaders of the Senate and the House and are members of the same party. But education issues were not always drawn along conventional political lines. Though I could generally count on a more cordial chair in the Republican Senate than in the Democratic House, the Republicans were split into moderates and extremists, and there was also controversy over the federal role in education. So some hostility could be expected even from the so-called friendly side of the aisle.

This congressional hearing procedure has grown out of two centuries of lawmaking, and the actual work of drafting new laws is delegated to these committees. It is in pursuit of that process that the tradition has evolved for members of the president's cabinet to appear before the appropriate committees to present the views of the administration. They are not the only witnesses, of course; scheduled hearings are announced in advance and experts outside of government are often requested to appear. This information is circulated widely. Indeed, congressional hearings are public procedures except for sensitive or security matters. Everything said and all written materials presented are on the record unless special action is taken during the hearing to go off the record.

In the hearings in which I appeared as the principal witness, I could usually count on representatives of most of the major education interest groups to be in the audience. The press was likely to be there too, because the battle had begun over the future of the federal role in education and because education policy enacted into law, and laws that appropriated federal education dollars, were matters of nationwide interest.

With a wary eye on the potential for news headlines, and with constant awareness of the written account that would be subsequently reviewed, quoted, and printed in the *Congressional Record* and utilized at later times, I learned to prepare with great care for these hearings, focusing not only on the content of my opening testimony, which I was required to deliver to the committee in advance of my appearance, but trying to anticipate any and all questions in the debate that followed.

A cabinet member is required to present himself before the committee at the appointed hour and take his seat in the witness chair. He can bring his staff along, but if he relies on them for many answers, it quickly becomes apparent that he is not prepared. The gossip following a hearing often swirls around the way a cabinet officer was roasted in the hearing room, beaten to a pulp because the argument presented was quickly torn apart.

(The strategy to use if you are ill prepared, and the members are well prepared and smelling blood, is to have a lengthy written statement and read it slowly. In this manner a great deal of time is consumed, and the time left for questioning is limited. But this is a familiar tactic, and there are limits to how often it can be used.)

A cabinet officer who is confident of his subject matter will usually start with a very short statement summarizing the lengthier prepared testimony and then turn the time back to the chair for questions. This is the preferred and admired approach, and I cannot recall any time during my four years in the cabinet when I ever read my full testimony. I submitted it for the record, outlined the main points in anticipation of the debate, and invited questions.

But no degree of preparation, however assiduous and thorough, ever made the process of testifying enjoyable for me. The tension was great and the hazards built into the procedure too formidable.

If the hearing is adversarial, the chair has the right to draw first blood from the witness. In fact, it was not uncommon in the House for the chair to make a statement, before turning the time over to me, that took the initiative on issues and was intended to put me on the defensive before I had opened my mouth. Using the written testimony it had received in advance, the committee staff equipped its members with data and questions for me; and on occasion the chair would rebut my material before I had a chance to present it. This was an especially common practice when the press was in attendance.

The second questioner was always the ranking member of the minority party. In House hearings I could always count on very aggressive questioning from the chair, sometimes followed by supportive or even leading questions from the ranking Republican on the committee. But not always. I can recall some very brutal sessions from which I departed feeling that I didn't have a friend on either side of the aisle.

There were almost always surprises: points, allegations, facts, and figures raised by the opposition. My staff would pass me hasty notes or send up suggestions on items I might have missed. All this was a classic exchange between the legislative and executive branches, and it was obviously exhilarating as well as trying to persuade congressional committees to support legislation or adopt budget levels advocated by the president and his cabinet.

But by the time all the committee members had had an opportunity to interrogate me, I was exhausted. It was a long and grueling procedure, though a necessary part of the legislative and appropriations process on the Hill.

I soon learned to evaluate three different levels of interest House and Senate members brought to education legislation. The first was specific and transient: pressure a lawmaker brought to bear on me because a constituent with a particular concern had demanded that this be done. The second was specific but often surreptitious: the tendency, especially among senators, to tuck into appropriation bills special items for the benefit of a college or school back home. This is tantamount to having all the taxpayers of the nation, for example, put up the money to build a new library for a state university. The item is often concealed in the budget, but the senator gets an expression of intent buried in a committee report that no one really reads. Then, after the bill becomes law, he or she reads it to the cabinet officer and demands that the money be forked over.

Very different in kind was the commitment of the third level of interest, demonstrated by legislators who served on education subcommittees because they cared intensely about education and worked with great expertise to advance its cause.

That cause, and the citizens who benefit from it, have been well served by these dedicated and knowledgeable lawmakers in both houses of Congress. But their numbers are few; and unfortunately for my situation during the president's first term, liberals and moderates tended to serve on education committees while responsible conservatives gravitated to other areas of interest. Not all of them, of course; the able conservative senator from Utah, Orrin Hatch, was a notable exception. But the nation sorely needs to hear the voice of conservatives committed to education far more often in the process that establishes and funds federal education policy.

Confrontations in the committee hearing rooms were not the only or even the worst ones I had to contend with. Before I even got to the hearing, there was the matter of the Office of Management and Budget.

Since tax and spending cuts were the president's major concern, the hearings I testified at focused on proposed massive reductions in funds for education. Because of that concern, the administration required that all testimony to be presented to Congress be submitted first to OMB for review and comment and then returned to the submitting cabinet office. This reassured the administration that the departments were supporting its position, and it gave enormous power to OMB. In the early months of the president's first term, the zealots at OMB proposed some outrageous changes in the initial drafts of my testimony and generated some pitched battles between my staff and Stockman's.

When my prepared testimony was returned from OMB, I learned to expect editorial additions that had me questioning the need for guaranteed student loans, or attacking the necessity for the legislation that provided aid to handicapped students, or denying the need for vocational education funds.

The testimony was mine, and I was willing to represent and defend the president's policies whether or not I agreed with them. This goes with serving in his cabinet, and I accepted the responsibility. But this could be done without having the content sound shrill and dogmatic. The tone of the rhetoric and the general mood of my presentations had to be acceptable to me. I was not willing to let some ideologue at OMB tell me arrogantly what to say and how to say it when I testified before Congress.

It was very hard to lose these battles, and I lost so often that it became extremely difficult to be convincing in my appearances in hearings before Congress. I often found myself feeling that I should resign. I was frequently in a mutinous mood, and I grew very testy about OMB revisions of my written testimony. My behavior was not unlike that of a mean and rebellious younger child in a large family who receives frequent spankings from older children as well as parents. After a while I became numb and insensitive to all the pounding.

It was clear that the anti-Bell forces continued to be on the move. They gave wide circulation to what I proposed to say despite the fact that the material they received from ED was marked confidential. They used the drafts of my proposed opening statements to attack their favorite whipping boy, Bell, and his "liberal leanings."

In fact, this leaking of papers transmitted to Stockman's office became so flagrant that we devised a scheme of placing small code markings on all OMB-bound paperwork. By sending these only to OMB we were able to identify Xerox copies that ended up in the hands of the press. A reporter who worked for a conservative newspaper that was constantly taking shots at me asked what positions I was going to take at a crucial hearing scheduled early the next week. When I refused to comment, he showed me a copy of my draft. I snatched the paper out of his hands. There was the telltale evidence that he had received it from OMB.

My formal academic credentials in the field of economics began and ended with one lower-level college course. But I have read extensively about the central theories of supply-side economics. Furthermore, economics has been a real, not merely a theoretical, area for me over the years I have been involved in state and federal government and have debated tax and education budgets. I knew that if we were to achieve a healthy economy, we needed to do much more than cut taxes and slash expenditures. We needed to do more than provide incentives for business and industry to modernize their physical plants and install more efficient machinery and instruments of production. We needed to invest in our ultimate resource—human capital.

But that thinking never surfaced in OMB. The entire grand plan designed and piloted by Stockman was to cut taxes dramatically over a three-year period and to reduce federal expenditures by at least the amount sufficient to balance the budget prior to the 1984 election. Unlike some of his fellow supply-siders, Stockman did not believe that the economic growth stimulated by the Kemp-Roth tax cuts would generate sufficient revenue to achieve that balance. So he ripped into our departmental appropriations with fanatical intensity.

We listened to Stockman's economic gospel at almost every cabinet meeting. He prepared massive cuts in most department budgets except Defense. We talked about incentives for savings to stimulate capital formation. We compared our economic growth with the Japanese. We studied various schemes to pump more money into our outmoded manufacturing plants. We created tax structures to induce investment in new equipment.

We never lacked for reasons why we were in difficulty. Stockman and the other true believers identified all the drain and drag on the economy with the tax-eaters: people on welfare, those drawing unemployment insurance, students on loans and grants, farmers drawing subsidies, the elderly bleeding the public purse with Medicare, the poor exploiting Medicaid. We looked at charts and graphs until our heads were bulging with statistics. The culprits were the patrons of the welfare state. We were going to pull those leeches off the backs of decent, hardworking people.

But as any person knows if he or she is only half-bright and has watched the Congress for a length of time, many of Stockman's reductions in expenditures would inflict pain on the electorate, and this could not be done. Congress is unwilling to take action that hurts the voters who put them in office. Inflicting pain on a small segment of society is one thing, but multiple blows that pound on virtually every voter in the nation will not be delivered by the Senate and the House.

An experienced politician knows that change in our system takes time. It took five decades to build our hodgepodge of federal aid programs, and it will take more than one or two presidential terms to bring about the change that our Dave Stockman wanted to accomplish in four years. He tried as earnestly, pleadingly, and zealously as any ideologue could. But his boss was a realist and a master politician. Ronald Reagan knew that real revolution was not possible with the numbers we had in the House and Senate. He knew that our purpose was to exercise our powers of persuasion from the Oval Office and from the cabinet offices in the executive branch. The president proposes, congress disposes, and between proposal and disposal compromises occur. The president recognized that we would make our changes gradually and steadily. He would take a strong position and then trade for some middle ground. This was exasperating to Stockman and to radical-right critics outside the inner circle who labeled it with their favorite epithet, *pragmatism*. They would criticize the president when essential and inevitable compromises were made. And they would bludgeon his cabinet, who were the weaklings who caved in and who would not let Reagan be Reagan.

In those early months of the administration I never heard from anyone, regardless of which faction he or she belonged to, a single word about education. There were countless discussions about giving America new hope, strength, and confidence, but no one ever mentioned human capital formation and the need for skilled intelligence and bright and productive citizens. This was to my mind our most urgent need; change could not come about without it. We need to reform and renew our vast, decentralized education system to make that happen.

The heart of education is its teachers. If that reform was to get under way, it made sense to begin with the teachers. I thought about this even amid the tumult and the battles of those difficult months, because I knew what I wanted to do. I wanted to promote performance-based salaries for teachers. The profession was sinking along with student SAT scores. I had ideas from my own experience about how to cure both these ailments. A public forum was coming up that I could take advantage of. Budget wars or not, it was time to begin the effort.

CHAPTER 7

Career Ladders for America's Teachers

I knew that the teaching profession was in deep trouble. Morale was terrible. Salaries were dreadfully low. Respect for teachers was commensurate with their salaries. We needed to make teaching more attractive in the United States. The most talented college youth shunned our profession. Those who could make it in engineering, business, law, medicine, accounting, and other professions would not pass up these opportunities for a career in the classroom.

The teachers' organizations insisted that teachers be paid on a schedule that was based on each teacher's years of experience, college degrees, and credits earned. All teachers, for example, who had five years of experience, a baccalaureate degree, and fifteen credits or semester hours of graduate work would get identical salaries in a school system operating on a single salary schedule. There was no recognition for distinguished teaching performance. The only promotions were in school administration. Thus, many outstanding teachers left the classrooms in which they had performed with great distinction to become mediocre school principals. Others left education altogether to seek more promising opportunities elsewhere.

One of the highest priorities during all my years in education has been to provide leadership in building a truly great teaching profession. Our schools' performance deficiencies can be traced directly to the pitiful standing of teachers in American society. Many people claim that the teachers are to blame. It is the teachers who insist on paying the least at the level of the best, and it is their unions that force taxpayers to raise the salaries of the worst at the same rate as the best in order to pay the best what they are worth. This indictment may be a bit unfair, but it does identify the most serious obstacle to bringing better talent into the classroom. Teaching is a dead-end job.

I found my opportunity to speak out about this problem to a target audience when I gave the keynote address at a meeting of the Southern Association of Colleges and Schools in Atlanta in 1982. Following my speech, the *Atlanta Constitution* told its readers: "U.S. Education Secretary Terrel H. Bell raised the heated issue of merit pay for public school teachers in Atlanta Monday by touting his master teacher proposal before a group of Southern educators. His plan would change the system of paying all public school teachers a standard salary and create a series of career ladder steps. . . ."

The speech before this large and prestigious association provoked a sharp response from teachers' organizations. The story was picked up by the wire services. It eventually became a nationwide issue. I came back to it many times. I had selected the South as an ideal place to launch my campaign because its states pay the lowest salaries, and I knew that the emerging new South wanted more effective schools.

In this address I compared the opportunities for promotion among college professors with those of elementary and secondary school teachers. Almost without exception, colleges and universities have a system of academic rank on their campuses. A young Ph.D. usually starts out as an assistant professor. By meeting criteria for promotion, and after being evaluated by a panel of peers and administrators, the academic professional on a college campus may move up a career ladder to associate and full professor levels. Recently this system of advancement has been enhanced by distinguished professorships and endowed chairs that provide additional recognition and reward to those who have attained eminence in their disciplines.

Though this system is certainly not perfect, it has sought to meet the need of bright and creative college teachers, researchers, and scholars to find fulfillment in their work. By contrast, the public and private elementary and high schools have doggedly refused to reward excellence and punish mediocrity in teaching.

Like other members of the Reagan cabinet, I had many opportunities to speak at conventions and other meetings. There were numerous interviews with the press and appearances on television as well. At most of these events I was alert for occasions where I could highlight the low standing of teachers in our society. I would compare the system of academic rank and promotion opportunities in higher education with the absence of any type of career ladder for teachers in our elementary and secondary schools.

All through 1982, I focused on the teacher compensation promotion issue whenever I addressed meetings of school boards, administrators, and teachers' organizations. Opponents were numerous.

Many teachers' organizations insisted it was impossible to measure teaching effectiveness. They said that administrators would use the career-ladder system to punish teachers. Merit pay had been tried before, and it had failed.

I had answers to these criticisms. The colleges had been able to meet problems such as these. They involved the faculty in the process. They had the candidates' peers serve on panels that reviewed applications for promotion and made recommendations. It was hard to find a college or university that did not have a career-ladder system of academic rank. If it was so horrible, why had higher education embraced it with such fervor for decades? I acknowledged that the proposed career-ladder system for teachers would not be perfect. Mistakes would be made just as they had been in higher education. But we *had* to change the system of rewards, recognition, and promotion of teachers. The dreadful sameness of a single salary schedule and fixed compensation had to go. It was like looking up the price of a train ticket to Chicago.

I proposed that the position of master teacher in the elementary and secondary levels of education become the schools' equivalent to the rank of full professor on the university campus. We were not competing effectively in the human talent marketplace. We would never build a truly great teaching profession until we met this serious deficiency that was a plague on teachers and students alike.

The nation's largest teachers' union, the National Education Association, attacked me by citing a litany of failures, when merit pay had to be junked. They reminded me that I had tried it myself in my early career as a superintendent of schools in Ogden, Utah, and I had failed miserably.

This rebuttal touched a sad and sore point. Eager to pay distinguished teachers for the outstanding contributions they made to their communities, I had established a merit pay system while I was superintendent of schools in Weber County, Ogden, Utah, in the early 1960s. It did go down in ruins. But the system itself was inherently successful. We lost in the political arena. The memory will always be painful.

I had come to Ogden from Wyoming, where I was superintendent of the Star Valley school system. I was surprised to find in the Utah school laws an incentive program enacted by the legislature to encourage school systems to pay their teachers on a merit basis. You could claim additional state money in the finance formula if you offered a merit pay system.

Utah has only forty school districts, and the Utah Society of School Superintendents had agreed to boycott the merit pay incentive system. This exclusive club of forty members had had an eight-year fight with conservative Governor J. Bracken Lee. Lee had pushed through his merit pay bill for teachers, but the school lobby had amended his bill to make participation optional. The superintendents had entered into a pact to ignore it.

After having served as a school superintendent in Idaho and Wyoming, I was convinced that the single salary schedule didn't do enough to attract and hold top teaching talent. Governor Lee's merit pay law was a happy surprise and an opportunity.

I put in my claim for the additional funds. My large, newly adopted school system was in the merit pay business.

We taught all our principals and supervisors in this large school system to use the Cornell Teacher Observation Instrument. We adopted the National Teacher Examination published by the Educational Testing Service of Princeton, New Jersey. We used a nationally standardized achievement test to measure student progress.

In keeping with the spirit of the merit pay law, we allowed every teacher to make individual decisions concerning his or her participation. This was the key to the success of the program. Teachers who objected were not compelled to be involved in the intensive evaluation, supervision, and testing process. They would remain on the standard salary schedule. The beauty of the arrangement was that funds in the regular budget were not used for the merit salary increases. Utah had wisely made separate provisions for this funding.

When I started to pay teachers additional money for distinguished teaching, there was intense public interest in the experiment. I was viewed as a young turk from Wyoming who had recently arrived in Ogden. But I was quickly targeted as a maverick and disapproved of by my fellow superintendents and the Utah Education Association, the state affiliate of the NEA.

As we handed out our first salary payments for outstanding teaching performance, we reached for all the press coverage we could get. The teachers were featured in the newspapers with photographs and headlines. We had broken through the barrier established by the union. It was widely known that in the Weber County schools extra effort and distinguished performance would be rewarded.

We honored our promise to the teachers that no one would be forced to participate. We also made no claims that we could make perfect measurements of teacher performance. We simply promised to be as fair, evenhanded, and objective as possible.

In the second year of the program I knew I had passed a critical point when the president of the local teachers' association applied for approval to participate in the program. Her name was Mable Blayney. She was a tough, salty, very able and dynamic high school English teacher. And up to then she had been a caustic critic of my merit pay programs.

Of course, Mable qualified for the performance-based bonus. All her scores were high, and we had a new convert fresh from the inner circle of the Utah Education Association. This came at a time when we were being widely attacked, and it made a tremendous difference to the political viability of our campaign to reform salary practices.

In an era of acute teacher shortages and a dreadfully inadequate supply of promising candidates to fill new positions in a fast-growing school district, we began to get an unusual number of applications from neighboring school systems. Most of these applicants were talented, capable teachers who were confident they could qualify under our merit pay standards. We joyfully picked up some of the best teachers among the ranks of other school systems.

Our competition cried in outrage. Talented, capable teachers were very hard to get. They were also very mobile, and I was surprised at how quickly we had created a magnet situation that was drawing able teachers into our system.

I had inherited a splendid group of administrators in Weber County. They had to be trained in the use of the Cornell Teacher Observation Instrument. They had to learn more about tests and measurements. It took hard work and additional time. They loved the challenge. We were getting attention. We were receiving accolades from the business community and the press. They were therefore motivated to try even harder. In every way, our venture into performance-based teacher salaries was a smashing success.

I felt that at long last I had found the key to strengthening the teaching profession. By rewarding outstanding performance we were getting greater effort. By highlighting exemplary teaching, we were finding increasing numbers of our professional staff aspiring to measure up to the best.

But the Utah teacher merit pay law was soon due to expire if not renewed. The Utah legislature also had to appropriate funds to keep the program going. It was at this point in my career that I learned a great lesson in legislative politics.

The Utah Education Association, the Utah Society of School Superintendents, and at least two-thirds of the local school boards had hatched a secret plan to murder our performance-based teacher pay program by shutting off its appropriations and killing the bill to renew the law. This situation was dangerous. The malicious merit system had to be wiped out before it spread to others. Our opponents had two choices of action: to implement their own program or to kill ours in the legislature. It seemed less painful to them to do the latter. There were thirty-nine school districts aligned against one maverick system that had dared to break stride. It would be easy to crush us, and that would settle the matter.

The center of political power was in Salt Lake City. The concentrated opposition to renewal and re-funding came from the largest metropolitan area of the state. But the fight in the Utah legislature was more than a local struggle in one of the smaller, remote states of the nation. The single salary schedule was widely accepted nationwide. One looked long and hard to find an exception to this practice, so our success had implications for the country as a whole.

We were no pushover in the struggle. I rallied the business community to our side. I found many sympathetic taxpayers, parents, and astute politicians ready to help. Our opponents were surprised at the effectiveness of our counterattack, and mounted a smear campaign. The emphasis was on my allegedly dictatorial tactics that had everyone in Weber County afraid to express opposition. It was claimed that our teachers hated the program. It was also said that our evaluation procedures were ill conceived and unfair. These charges swept through the legislative chambers in Salt Lake City, and we realized they were having an impact.

At this point I decided to risk everything on my standing with my faculty and administrative staff. I invited the legislative leadership to send staff members to Weber County to poll all teachers and administrators. All responses would be kept confidential, so no one need fear reprisals from me.

The invitation was accepted, and the results of the poll were both surprising and exhilarating. Two-thirds of those polled voted to keep the program going. Some said they were not entirely convinced that the program would ultimately succeed, but they wanted to continue with the effort. The majority responded that they liked our system of rewarding outstanding performance and they fully supported its continuation.

The following week our bill to renew and fund the Utah merit pay program passed the state senate by a substantial margin. I sat in the balcony with a tally sheet marking how each senator voted. There had been a caucus, several recesses, and much tugging and trading before the big victory.

Our big win in the senate came on Monday of the last week of the legislative session. In Utah, as in most small states, the sessions of the legislature are limited by constitutional mandate to a specified number of days. Utah's legislature was about to adjourn, so we had a big hurdle to get over if the bill was to pass the house in time.

The house speaker was a strong ally of the Utah Education Association, and this added to my apprehensiveness. He was under great pressure to keep the bill bottled up in committee. But the pressure from our side was equally intense. The fight had attracted statewide attention, and our support was growing every day. The major newspapers called for the continuation of the program. Even some doubters wanted to see it carried to conclusion to test its viability.

The next day, Tuesday, the bill was sent back to the senate for some technical amendments. This added some more points to my blood pressure, for I feared another protracted fight on the senate floor. But these worries were groundless, and the senate acted by routine voice vote. They had settled the matter earlier. Even its opponents wanted no more of the fight.

At this juncture, two strange, unrelated events clouded the outcome. The clerk of the house kept telling me to persuade his counterpart in the senate to hasten the transmittal of the bill so the house could act on it. The clerk of the senate assured me he *had* sent the bill over within minutes after the technical amendments had been acted on. He told me that Speaker of the House Ernest Dean was playing games with me. More precious time was lost while we searched futilely for the bill.

We were down to the last two days in the session when another actor entered the scene. The president of Brigham Young University, Dr. Ernest L. Wilkinson, decided I needed some help. He left his duties in Provo to come to my rescue.

Ernie Wilkinson was a very strong-willed, conservative Republican. He was a splendid man in many respects, but he was not known for his tact or charm. When he fixed his mind on an objective, he functioned like a bulldozer. He went straight ahead. Right was right and wrong was wrong. There were no shades of gray for Ernie. We wore the white hats. We were going to beat our black-hatted opponents to a pulp and shove the merit pay bill through the house.

The entrance of Dr. Wilkinson was welcomed by many of my supporters. Indeed, some of them, meaning well, had recruited him to finish the battle in glorious style. Unfortunately, Ernie Wilkinson hurt more than he helped. Several house members whose support we needed were outraged at his arm-twisting. They pleaded with me to send Ernie back to Provo. But no one could send Ernie anywhere, least of all the new school superintendent from Wyoming who was himself an anomaly in Utah.

So far as our great campaign for renewal of support of the merit pay law was concerned, the legislative session ended in chaos. Where was the bill? Who needed Ernie to complicate the situation? Both Earnest Dean and Ernest Wilkinson were from Utah County. They didn't admire each other. One was a liberal Democrat and the other a very conservative Republican. The battle of the two Ernies added intolerable emotion to an already tense situation. As a result, the legislature adjourned, as required by the constitution, and merit pay disappeared by default—my bill died, and the program was not funded.

A few days after the session adjourned, the mystery of the vanished bill was solved. Cleaning out desks in the house chamber, the legislative staff found it safely locked up in the long middle drawer of the Speaker's desk. A good friend who worked for the legislature called to tell me about it.

My first impulse was to rant and accuse. But for once in my passionate younger days I restrained myself and let the matter stand, since nothing could be done. Besides, given the emotions churned up by the other Ernie, the house was likely to have killed the bill. Our opposition had been gaining, and we were losing momentum when the session expired.

In the midst of his frustration over an issue in Congress, the late Hubert Humphrey once said that the process of lawmaking was like that of making sausage. In both instances one is better off not observing what goes in because it will surely upset the stomach. My recall of the loss of our merit pay bill in the Utah legislature made me sick for days thereafter.

All of us in the Weber County schools felt crushed and betrayed. The fine rhetoric from legislators about paying the best teachers more sounded hollow to us in the aftermath of that disastrous legislative session.

The Utah Education Association celebrated its victory. Their publications praised those legislators who opposed us and referred to our supporters as enemies of education who would surely be defeated in the next election.

But after a period of grief and soul-searching, I came upon another scheme to keep our program alive. Like many states, Utah law limits the millage the local school board can levy on property to finance schools. Our mill levy had been up to the maximum level for years. However, with a special election in which consent is obtained from the people, the school board may increase this levy. This procedure is called a school tax leeway election. I recommended to our board that we ask the people to fund the merit pay program through this special tax, and it approved my request. I had had so many phone calls, letters, and other expressions of sympathy for our loss that I was convinced the taxpayers would support us in this most worthy cause.

But once the election date was announced, the opposition gathered its forces. Once again the UEA opposed us. It was joined by taxpayer association groups. For the first time in my career, I found hostility coming from both the right and the left. Full-page ads were purchased in local newspapers. Antitax rallies were held throughout the county, a measure of the alarm the proposal generated among education leaders and teachers' groups. They had just concluded celebrating their big victory in the legislature, and here we were again offering the hated merit pay program through the back door of the tax leeway law. Our opponents tried to get a state attorney general's opinion that the leeway election would not be valid, and when they failed in this effort they tried to get a court order postponing the election. The courts upheld our position and the election was held on the appointed day.

I campaigned every day for our tax leeway. The opposition was a surprise to me, and the extent of it was totally unanticipated. We not only lost, we suffered a humiliating defeat. For every vote in favor, we had five voters against us.

I learned another hard lesson from the tax leeway election defeat: When it comes to increasing taxes, even the most faithful supporters of schools often join with opponents to defeat a worthy cause. Faced with a choice between the pocketbook and good education, many parents choose the former.

It was clear to me that I had no choice but to leave the Weber County Schools. I accepted a professorship at Utah State University and resolved to live the quiet life of a scholar-teacher.

But this resolution was short lived. The Utah State Board of Education asked me to become state superintendent of public instruction. Humanly pleased by the knowledge that the UEA would be shocked at my appointment, I accepted. As the chief state school officer, I assumed my new duties in June 1963. I was in a position to represent the entire statewide public school system before the legislature. I had control over teacher certification and teacher education. I relished the fresh opportunity to get back into the fight for change and reform.

The chance for action came more quickly than I expected because the state was in a crisis over school funding when I took over. In response to a threat by the UEA of a statewide school strike the previous September, Governor George Dewey Clyde had appointed a study commission to appraise the adequacy of the financial support the state was providing its schools. The union agreed to hold the strike in abeyance until the commission came in with its findings. The governor promised that he would call a special session of the legislature to consider increased funding if the report recommended it.

Governor Clyde's commission delivered its report in mid-May of 1964, with only two weeks remaining in the school year. The report highlighted many serious deficiencies in the schools that could only be corrected by appropriating additional funds.

The governor promptly rejected the findings of his own commission. Since he had promised that he would call a special session of the legislature if the study he proposed recommended it, the teachers were justifiably outraged. The UEA called a mass meeting of its members and went on strike. Thus, before the end of my first year in office, we had the first statewide teachers' strike in the history of the nation.

The weekend before the strike was the longest one in my memory. The school districts had filed their calendars with my office, indicating which days school would be in session. The teachers were under contract to teach those days.

School boards and local superintendents called me. What could they do? If the local school boards amended the calendar, they would be supporting or accommodating the strike. What should they do if some teachers reported to work while others supported the strike? If the school boards closed the schools in response to a threatened strike, and if loyal teachers reported to work to find the schools shut down, they could then find solid legal ground for charging the school districts with breach of their contracts.

I reasoned that the UEA announcement of a strike would not be supported statewide. I felt confident that most of the teachers would report to work Monday. We couldn't let them down by closing our schools just because UEA said its members would not be teaching Monday.

I admonished every school district to open school Monday. I went on television to announce to the public that schools would be open as usual. For those teachers who did not show up we would have substitutes. I called on parents to support us in this crisis.

But the teachers were so furious over the governor's broken promise that even the least militant of the UEA membership largely joined in the walkout.

The strike lasted for a week. After another mass meeting of teachers the following Saturday, Utah's schools were opened, and we had a relatively orderly conclusion of the academic year.

My experience with merit pay and the statewide teachers' strike taught me to be less trusting, more wary, and much more perceptive about pressures and their impact on those in elective office. The quest to establish a perception of strength and power overrides almost everything else that a politician does. To win office and hold it are paramount.

My dismay at the sight of teachers walking picket lines was part of my attaining a bit more political and intellectual maturity. I had to admit that our schools received more support after the big walkout. I also realized that because people were more tolerant and understanding of the teachers' reasons for supporting the strike, it was not the end of the line as far as public support of teachers was concerned.

I never changed my view that the UEA and NEA policies on merit pay and career ladders were harmful to the ultimate advancement of the teaching profession. But I did become more understanding of the militancy of today's teachers. Like other groups, they have the right to organize and exert the weight and influence of their numbers to advance their interests. At the same time that I argue that teachers' strikes have not been very effective, I must concede that the biggest one in which I had a role did result in some good as well as harm.

Major changes in society have altered the nature of schools, and this has made the teacher's job more difficult. In our urban centers we have large non-English-speaking student populations. As the middle class has fled to the suburbs, we have witnessed the ghettoization of many neighborhoods. This has compounded the problems—and the quality—of education in most of our cities. Poverty, teenage pregnancy, drugs, one-parent households, illiteracy, and a sense of hopelessness have all contributed to the shocking declines in the quality of schools and schooling. The comparative stability of home, family, and before- and after-school environment that only a generation or so ago were the norm, and that are so crucial to student achievement, have been widely eroded—to the detriment of teaching and learning.

To be a teacher today is very different from what it once was. Not only is the task of teaching itself more complex, difficult, and often frustrating; it is compounded by low pay, scorned status, and lack of reward for excellence. It is no wonder morale has dropped catastrophically; it is no wonder that our best and brightest young people, whose minds and imaginations could bring both discipline and innovation to the classroom, seek their careers elsewhere.

I was convinced that we could change the regard in which teachers are held and the quality of education if we restored to the profession the esteem and rewards that once were its due. So I came back to the issues of career ladders and merit pay every time I could, in speeches and interviews and informal meetings. It seemed to be working. Certainly the subject was touching a popular chord; I could tell that from the attention it drew, not only in letters and publicity and newspaper articles but from eruptions of disquiet in the NEA. That was fine. Tranquility does not breed change.

CHAPTER 8

The Abolitionists Fail to Abolish Education

||||||||||||||||||||||||||||||||||||||||||||||||||||||||||||||||||||||||||||||||||||||||||||||||||||||||||||||||||||||||||||||||||||||||||||||||||||||||||||||

To my surprise and pleasure, the attention my drive for merit pay had drawn, and the widely noted departures of Curran, Sweet, Oliver, and Beard, turned the inconsequential secretary of education into a more significant figure—at least outside the West Wing. The July 27, 1982, issue of *U.S. News & World Report* published a survey and appraisal of cabinet member effectiveness, with all thirteen of our faces pictured on the cover. We were placed in order of ranking according to how "131 Washington Insiders" had rated us. On a ten-point rating scale, this is how we came out:

1. Regan (Treasury)	8.8
2. Lewis (Transportation)	8.3
3. Weinberger (Defense)	7.5
4. Haig (State)	7.3
5. Bell (Education)	7.0
6. Baldridge (Commerce)	6.7
7. Watt (Interior)	6.6
8. Block (Agriculture)	6.4
9. Smith (Justice)	5.4
10. Schweiker (Health & Human Services)	5.1
11. Pierce (Housing & Urban Development)	4.9
12. Edwards (Energy)	4.4
13. Donovan (Labor)	4.3

The article inside discussed me as "the highly regarded dark horse in the Reagan cabinet." The magazine speculated that "the ultimate surprise would be if Bell's Education Department, which has been slated for eventual elimination in Reagan's drive to trim the bureaucracy, escapes the ax—something that now seems a distinct possibility." "If it does," the article concluded, "many in Washington will credit—or blame— the Education Secretary."

The article pleased me, obviously, but more important, it came at the best possible moment. I needed time, and this made a contribution by giving me some valuable credibility in Washington.

I never argued on behalf of education to any group before which I might appear to be disloyal. The president did encourage private debate before issues were decided, and I tried to use this to advantage. But the *U.S. News* piece gave me a warning for even greater discretion when it said, "The Secretary's supporters say Bell has spared the department some intended cuts through effective lobbying at the White House."

I heard the message. It was especially important because it was time to meet my obligation to replace the Department of Education with a foundation type of structure. I had asked for this assignment in my preappointment interview at Blair House to ensure the best possible federal role for education in the changeover; but my tenure in the cabinet had me more and more convinced that cabinet status was crucial. I had experienced firsthand the advantages of having access to the president, the senior White House staff, the OMB director, and the other secretaries at cabinet meetings and at other times as well. But I had to keep this conviction to myself. I had a commitment to the president.

From the time I met with Ed Meese and Penn James in San Diego to now, the time to draft the actual bill, I had anticipated administration support for the foundation concept that Meese had generated by early January 1981. I meant to keep my promise, but I was determined to fight for as strong a federal role for education in this new entity as possible.

From all the hassles over staff and the plotting that had gone on, I felt that I had grown more astute about how the White House staff and the president worked to fulfill their own agendas. But as the bill to abolish ED proved, I still had a lot to learn.

I wanted to retain most of the existing federal programs in the new foundation. This included the vital college-student-aid funding from loans, work-study opportunities, and grants to financially needy students. It also encompassed supplemental financial assistance to school districts to comply with strict federal laws compelling them to meet the educational needs of handicapped children. Title I, the single largest federal aid program, which provided special education services to children in schools where there were heavy concentrations of low-income and educationally disadvantaged pupils, had to be maintained and even strengthened, if politically possible. I also wanted to keep other smaller but essential programs of assistance such as bilingual education services to limited-English-proficient children and financial aid to school districts under federal desegregation court orders. I knew it was important to keep our educational research arm (NIE) and improve its services. Last, civil rights enforcement should be retained in the new agency if we were to keep faith with the promises of equal educational opportunity for minorities, the handicapped, and women. To maintain all this in the climate of abolishing and cutting was a tall order, but I knew I could do nothing less as we drafted our new law.

I attended a series of meetings chaired by Ed Meese and set up at the White House to seek consensus on the bill that we would introduce in Congress to abolish my department and create the foundation entity in its stead. The White House Office of Policy Development (OPD) was heavily involved in these sessions because this was the unit set up in the Reagan administration to oversee new policy initiatives.

The OPD was under the administrative direction of Martin Anderson. Marty came from the Hoover Institute in California. The thinking in his office was to abolish the federal role in education research and shut down NIE. Marty also wanted gradually to phase out virtually every program of financial assistance to schools and colleges. He objected to my position as too liberal and not fully commensurate with the president's intent.

Meese's plan would scatter the federal education assistance programs all over town by placing aid responsibilities in Labor, Commerce, Health and Human Services, and Treasury. He would shut down our Office of Civil Rights and assign the role of civil rights enforcement to the Department of Justice. The main purpose of the Meese proposals was to make it more difficult for education lobbyists to influence decisions made in the federal bureaucracy. By dispersing the programs in many agencies, educational organizations would be forced to report to and work with several cabinet agencies, and this would complicate and frustrate their efforts.

We clashed on these ideas. We met numerous times, and I heard their rationale time and again; but it did not make sense, and I remained adamant. I could see no reason for scattering responsibility for education all over the bureaucracy as Meese wanted, and I could not agree to the deep retrenchment that Marty advocated.

I argued that their ideas would not work because the laws we administered required coordination of grant approvals and fund allocations to schools and colleges to ensure that recipients of federal dollars were accredited as required by law and that they also complied with all the civil rights laws. We worked with state education agencies to coordinate these approvals; to force these units of state government to seek approvals in five separate federal departments would create an administrative nightmare. Savvy lawmakers who held hearings on a bill with these proposals would find it a great opportunity to ridicule the president publicly.

All these points were telling arguments from my side of the discussion, and I was persuasive enough to get Anderson and Meese to accede grudgingly to the compromise draft we finally ended up with. Moreover, since I would be the prime witness in Congress on these proposals, I had to be in a position to argue the administration's view with at least some degree of credibility.

The bill we finally agreed to submit to the cabinet and the president kept the traditional federal role of providing college student aid, supplemental assistance for handicapped and disadvantaged students, and most of the other programs—including educational research—in the proposed foundation. I lost on the issue of retaining civil rights enforcement; this responsibility would go to the Department of Justice. I could only concede that the bill we agreed on was less dreadful than what either Meese or Anderson wanted.

The next step in the procedure was to present the bill to the Cabinet Council on Human Resources, chaired by Secretary of Health and Human Services Schweiker. The council members were the secretaries of labor, agriculture, HUD, justice, and ED. The review by this body was easy. We explained the rationale. Meese said it was an interim measure until we could phase out all federal spending for education. This did not surprise me, because he had expressed these views when I first met him. However, this was not my intent, and I knew that the president did not want to go that far, but I kept quiet. The purpose now was to get council approval of the bill. I would fight the other fight if and when we came to it.

By January of 1982 our proposal was ready for presentation to the full cabinet. We had a prominent place on the crowded agenda of a cabinet meeting. Thomas Jefferson's portrait looking down on the cabinet table reminded me of his famous statement that education was essential to the future of freedom and of the Republic, and there we sat denigrating education. But, then, Jefferson also advocated that the states carry the ball on education, so perhaps he did not turn over in his grave when I presented the draft legislation to abolish ED.

During the cabinet meeting I studied the president's reactions intently to pick up any hints of dissatisfaction. I had made a commitment to him to change the structure of ED, and I wanted assurance that this proposal filled the bill.

My guess was that Ed Meese had discussed this matter with the president beforehand, and if he had reported the difficult time we had had and how I had resisted his proposals, this would come out in Ronald Reagan's response. The president expressed no objections whatsoever, nor could I detect any reluctance or disappointment on his part.

I was also interested in any reactions Cap Weinberger might have. Since he had been my former boss when he was secretary of the old Department of Health, Education, and Welfare, I wondered if Cap would express a strong preference for putting the *E* back in HEW. This was the last thing I wanted, and I was on edge about it. I noted that he was unusually quiet about the entire matter. He expressed no opposition, but neither did he display enthusiasm.

The next move after cabinet approval was the major hurdle of getting the proposed new law enacted by Congress. This would be a tall order. After the cabinet heard the proposal, the president suggested that we introduce the bill in the Senate, where we had a Republican majority and our party chaired the committee hearing sessions. I had to go to Senate Majority Leader Howard Baker and then to Chairman of the Senate Government Operations Committee William Roth. I prepared carefully for my meetings with them. I did not want anyone to be able to accuse me of failing to meet my commitment to the president.

I decided to start my campaign for Senate approval with Howard Baker. Baker was a moderate Republican. The educators in his home state of Tennessee were close to him because he had been a solid supporter of education appropriations and most of the recent legislation enacted by Congress. He was very knowledgeable about the problems faced by schools and colleges.

I had to catch Baker between meetings on the Hill. He was a very busy man laboring under many pressures. The Republican majority in the Senate was slim, and he had to work constantly with the House side, where the Democrats were in firm control.

When I finally caught a few minutes with him, I tried to give him my very best explanation of the rationale for our proposal. I explained the president's concern about federal control of schools and colleges. I described the power of cabinet officers to promulgate regulations and to go beyond legislation. I explained that a foundation was an ideal organization for education on the federal level. Foundations give financial assistance to others who are in charge. They usually do not take over and run things as line agencies in the government are inclined to do. Then I appealed to his loyalty to the Republican Party, and to our 1980 platform that had called for abolishing ED. Finally, I explained that the president wanted this legislation and that we were looking to him as majority leader to push our administration's program through Congress.

Baker listened politely, smiling from time to time as I gave him my sales talk. When I had finished, he leaned back, looked at me sideways, and gave his response: "We can't abolish the Department of Education. We just went through a big fight a couple of years ago to establish it."

"We need effective leadership for education on the federal level," I said. "We can have that without federal control. The laws have been carefully written to prohibit federal control."

"You made a good pitch. You've done your part. But I don't think you really believe it." He smiled as he said this. He not only refused to push the bill but he promised to fight the proposal with all his might.

I left Howard Baker's office surprised by his stand and concerned about how effectively I had conveyed my commitment to the president. Baker was obviously right about my lukewarm enthusiasm for abolishing ED, but I had certainly not meant my feeling to show. Since I had begun to understand the importance of keeping education's seat at the cabinet table, I wondered about the quality of my presentation. Was I being sufficiently sincere? I worked for the president. I knew where he stood on the future of ED. I also tried to keep foremost in my mind that I had an obligation either to support him or to resign. Was I coming across as reluctant? How could I serve him feeling as I increasingly did about keeping ED as it was?

I had debated the issues on the proposed legislation. The proposal was a compromise between my position and that of Ed Meese and Marty Anderson. They had yielded on a number of significant points. It was inevitable that we present a bill to Congress carrying out the president's campaign promise. The draft legislation that I gave to Howard Baker represented that commitment, yet I left his office knowing that he wouldn't even read the bill, much less support it.

When I followed up with Howard Baker's staff I was assured that his decision was firm. Not only would he not help to pass it, he had meant it when he said he was going to oppose the bill actively.

I reported to the president that I couldn't win Howard Baker's support. Ronald Reagan was not discouraged: "Don't worry about it, Ted, I'll talk to Howard," he assured me.

Two weeks later I asked the president if he had had that talk. He had, and he told me that he had never seen Baker so stubborn on any issue.

The chairman of the Senate Government Operations Committee, William Roth of Delaware, was the object of my next selling effort. Because he was cosponsor of a key piece of conservative legislation, the Kemp-Roth bill, and its supply-side economics program, I expected him to be eager to support my legislation. Having failed with Baker, I made additional preparations before approaching Roth.

But he was surprisingly tough. He attacked the rationale of the bill. He knew much of the history of the bill that had created the department. Before I could even finish, he was giving me the other side of the argument, and he dumped on me and my bill so heavily that I could see it would be futile to ask him to sponsor it. Roth explained that he was a fiscal conservative but a strong supporter of education. He told me that there was an important federal role in education and he favored keeping a cabinet-level ED.

Not only did I fail to win support from the two Senate leaders I had hoped would sponsor the bill, but I received a promise of opposition from the majority leader and the chairman of the committee that would conduct the hearings.

By this time the bill's provisions had appeared in the press. The reaction from most of the education associations was swift and predictable. Even organizations that had opposed the creation of ED, such as the American Federation of Teachers, refused to support our legislation.

I went over to the House side to seek endorsements there. Senator Roth's counterpart, Chairman Brooks of the House Government Operations Committee, gave me a lively rebuttal. His points were well taken. My baby was ugly. Why not drop the whole thing?

I went from Brooks to see my good friend, Representative Trent Lott of Mississippi. Trent was a conservative Republican, very bright and articulate, and a solid supporter of Reagan legislation. He was a very popular man in his home congressional district. Being a Republican in Mississippi took courage and masterly political skill. I was confident that Trent would not only support me but give me some sound advice.

Trent explained to me how many members of his own family had been teachers. He went to some lengths to explain how important education was. The bottom line of our conversation was that Trent agreed with all the others. He had no enthusiasm for abolishing the Department of Education.

Before I was done, I had gone to virtually every member of the U.S. Senate on both sides of the aisle. The only exceptions were a small number of senators who I knew beyond any doubt would oppose me. I worked hard with one-on-one contacts. I kept a list of senators I had contacted on the back of an envelope that I carried in my pocket. After all my contacts, I consulted this list. The most optimistic estimate I could make was that nineteen senators would support the president's bill to abolish ED and establish a foundation in its stead. Eighty-one would vote against it.

This situation reminded me of a quip the late Dr. Edna Snow Cannon used to use when we tried to get legislation passed in the Utah legislature. She added one to the Bible's beatitudes, "Blessed are they who expect nothing, for they shall not be disappointed." I had reached that point in my effort to fulfill the president's promise.

I had known that the bill would meet stiff opposition, but I had no idea that it would smash into so many stone walls. It was controversial legislation. Moreover, the Congress had plenty of controversy before it at that point.

In politics, when you have to take a stand on an issue on which there are divided views and strong feelings, it is difficult to come out a winner. You gain from those who agree with the position you ultimately take, but you also pick up enemies among those who have strong feelings and deep resentment. As you confront such issues, you gradually accumulate a backyard full of snipers. In lawmaking these issues must eventually be confronted with a yes or no vote. The side opposing your position reports the results back home in newsletters to its constituents. If you are a politician, why get into needless controversy? Even if you tend to lean in one direction, you must carefully weigh the opposition and its potential for adding more snipers around your political backyard.

This truism of political decision making mitigated against our bill to abolish ED. Why take a stand on this and make all the teachers, teachers' families, and half the PTA members back home angry at you? How many supporters will you get from the other side? The political hazards far outweighed any potential for political gain. I had a difficult package to sell.

A few short years earlier Jimmy Carter had pressed with all his political skill to push through the bill creating ED. It was a controversial move, but he had his staff give it high priority. The huge National Education Association and a dozen other education associations were behind him. President Carter had promised to create a separate Department of Education, and with the 1980 election coming up he again needed support from the education community. The bill passed the House with a margin of only four votes. It was a source of heated debate in the

Senate before its passage there. The memory of the tension and emotion surrounding this was still strong in both chambers. This was another reason the bill I was trying to sell on the Hill was unwelcome. They had been through that bruising fight. Why bring it up again?

The reaction to the administration's bill by the movement conservatives was predictable. They didn't want to keep any semblance of the Department of Education whatever its form. Our proposal was simply not acceptable. The most extreme among them wanted to abolish ED and cut out every dime of federal expenditures for education. To them, the bill to create a foundation was simply an excuse to keep the Department of Education under another name.

So their reaction was quick, unequivocal, and violent. Their presses rolled out the rhetoric against the bill. But they never tied it to Ed Meese or Ronald Reagan; that would not serve their ends. The proposed bill was all my handiwork.

To their minds, this was ample proof of my infidelity to conservative philosophy and to Ronald Reagan's program. If there was ever proof that I had to go, this was it! Many of them knew that I was supporting the president's position on this matter; they simply misused Reagan's position for their own ends.

Liberals and moderates did not like the foundation idea for different reasons. They wanted to keep the department. They would have no part of the foundation concept. Education should be represented in Washington at the cabinet level. Liberals wanted to expand the federal role and invest more money. Moderates wanted to hold the line, but they too were convinced that we should not abolish ED.

The Reagan administration had put together a proposal that was impartial: It made all sides equally angry. It also reflected our political ineptitude. I knew the bill would be hard to pass, but at least I wanted the debate to establish a respectable record that would highlight the president's views.

I had watched the president fight uphill battles for other critical conservative causes. I expected him to use his considerable weight to give this legislation that fulfilled his campaign promise a similar push. After all, the commitment was the president's, not mine. We had agreed that we would strike a middle posture between total abolition on the one hand and extension of full support of ED on the other. The bill we drafted did that. It preserved the federal role, and it met the president's campaign commitment.

One of the time-honored practices in Washington power circles is distancing. When an unpopular issue or an absolutely certain loser appears on the scene, you distance yourself from it or from the individual. The "it" in this matter was the foundation proposal, and the person was Terrel Bell. To my dismay and bitterness, the foundation bill was mine. No one else owned it. It was a bastard child, and I was the father. The best thing to do was establish as much distance from both as possible.

In my many heated exchanges over the abortive bill, I failed to heed the advice I had heard years ago: "When arguing with a fool, make certain that he is not similarly occupied!" I was defending the indefensible; I was arguing with both the wise and the foolish.

CHAPTER 9

Justice for Whom?

IIIIIIIIIIIIIIIIIIIIIIIIIIIIIIIIIIIIIIIIIIIIIIIIIIIIIIIIIIIIIIIIIIIIIIIIIIIIIIIIIIIIIIIIIIIIIIIIIIIIIIIIIIIIIIIIIIIIIIIIIIIIIIIIIIIIIIIIIIIIIIIIIIIIIIII

In an effort to air gripes and defuse explosive tensions during the president's first term, Ed Meese sponsored a series of cabinet breakfasts at the White House. These were off-the-record sessions that enabled all thirteen cabinet members to meet with Ed to talk over problems and to ventilate issues that were particularly galling to us. It was a very effective procedure, and Ed performed his role well.

We usually met at about 7:30 A.M. on Wednesday mornings. Neither the president nor any of his other top staff members were present. I seldom had much to say at these cabinet breakfast sessions. I doubted that there was much value in expressing my frustrations to my twelve colleagues, and I didn't care to unload on Meese, so I listened to the others and learned all I could in silence. Meese would go around the cabinet table, and when he came to me I simply said that I had nothing to bring before the group. We heard mostly from the big four: State, Treasury, Defense, and Justice. I attended to keep in touch, and the sensitive matters often gave me clues that helped me to deal with the White House and OMB.

In January 1983, as we entered our third year in office, there was another cabinet breakfast at which Meese gave each of us copies of a new book just published by the Heritage Foundation. It was a sequel to the widely quoted *Mandate for Leadership* that Heritage put out immediately after the president was elected in 1980.

Meese had read it, and he advised us to scrutinize those sections that contained recommendations for our particular departments. These had timely advice for what should happen over the last two years of the president's first term. Riding from the White House back to my office, I opened the book to the section on education. The first paragraph stated that the first and foremost task for ED was for the president to fire the secretary. Without this, education in the Reagan administration would never assume its proper role.

Given my failure to abolish ED and Meese's role in the ill-fated foundation plan, I thought it was entirely appropriate for him to give me a complimentary copy of the new Heritage book. My only regret was that in my excitement at receiving the book I had failed to ask him to autograph it.

Actually, at that point, the conclusion of two years in the cabinet, it appeared to me that my departure was a good idea. I told my chief of staff, Elam Hertzler, in confidence that I planned to leave before too long, and he left Washington for a school superintendent's job in Oklahoma. A longtime friend, Thomas Anderson, moved up to the Hertzler position.

The original cabinet ranks began to thin out. Drew Lewis of Transportation had already left. Jim Edwards of Energy took a university executive job in South Carolina. Dick Schweiker of Health and Human Services became an insurance association executive. Al Haig had lasted no longer than eighteen months at State.

But before I left on my own initiative I had some urgent unfinished business that would require my presence for at least another three to six months.

The Justice Department was determined to weaken civil rights enforcement in the nation's colleges and schools, and I was not going to depart until I had—I hoped—altered that agenda.

Attorney General William French Smith, like Ed Meese who succeeded him in President Reagan's second term, wanted to change some time-honored practices in the federal government with respect to enforcement of the civil rights laws.

Smith and I met with Meese over a difference of view concerning the position the Reagan administration should take in the U.S. Supreme Court case of *Grove City College* v. *Bell*. We had been struggling for months over the interpretation of words in the civil rights laws, regulations promulgating these laws, and even over the meaning of sentences and phrases in the Constitution. Prior to the meeting in the West Wing, most of these discussions had taken place in my office, and they involved the attorney general's subordinates. Assistant Attorney General William Bradford Reynolds was usually the spokesman for Justice, and my assistant secretary for civil rights, Harry Singleton, often disagreed with him.

Those of us in the Department of Education were reasonably happy with the interpretations that had been established in prior years, and Reynolds seemed to be reaching for narrower, more restrictive reading of the laws.

The basis for these laws and regulations is, of course, the Fourteenth Amendment to the Constitution (1868):

> Section I. All persons born or naturalized in the United States, subject to the jurisdiction thereof, are citizens of the United States and of the state wherein they reside. No state shall make or enforce any law which shall abridge the privileges or immunities of citizens of the United States; nor shall any state deprive any person of life, liberty, or property, without due process of law, nor deny to any person within its jurisdiction the equal protection of the laws.

For generations, especially in the South, equal rights under the law had not meant that schools had to be open equally to white and black children. That interpretation, which led to "separate but equal" schools for the races in many states, had been established in a decision handed down by the U.S. Supreme Court. Action to abolish the practice of operating racially segregated schools was compelled by the famous Supreme Court decision in *Brown* v. *Board of Education of Topeka, Kansas.*

This decision held that operating "separate but equal" schools was unlawful. The existence of school segregation, with whites attending one set of schools and blacks attending schools specifically designated as institutions to be operated exclusively for them, ultimately compelled the integration of all public schools.

Court-ordered and supervised desegregation was a huge step for the schools, communities, and people of the South. It took about sixteen years after the *Brown* decision for the school districts in the South to comply fully with the intent of the Supreme Court.

Following this landmark U.S. Supreme Court civil rights decision, the Congress enacted supporting statutes. A series of civil rights laws that concentrated on eliminating racial discrimination came first, with the Civil Rights Act of 1964 being the most compelling and unambiguous statute. Then, federal legislation followed to ensure equal educational opportunity for the handicapped and to prohibit discrimination on the basis of sex. In these statutes Congress mandated that enforcement action be taken by the executive branch following certain hearings and other procedures to assure rights of appeal. Most of the major government agencies received funds for additional staff and mandates from Congress to receive and investigate complaints. Offices of Civil Rights in Justice, ED, and other agencies were staffed and funded.

Enforcement of civil rights laws through the years has been difficult because of ambiguities in the language of the laws themselves and also because of the decentralized control and management of educational institutions. Schools and colleges are both public and private, and the public ones are under the jurisdiction of state and local boards and administrators. These officials are, of course, sensitive to local public opinion, and federal intervention was often met with resistance.

Without equivocating about the outcome, it was important for federal officials in the judicial and executive branches of government to work with diplomacy and tact to gain, as much as possible, the support and good will of local and state officers. All too often, diplomacy and tact were lacking.

In past years the federal government had, in my view, often been heavy handed and disruptive in its zeal to bring about compliance with civil rights statutes. I agreed with many of the conservatives, including some of my critics in the Reagan administration, that there had been overreaching in the executive branch enforcement in the past. Some demands were not reasonable with respect to the time allowed to comply or the racial balance required.

In deciding when a school system or college is in compliance, for example, must each school have a student population with the same racial mix as the population of the school district as a whole? Must the classes inside the school also be racially balanced? For example, if the general population of a school district is 60 percent white, 30 percent black, and 10 percent Hispanic, must all schools reflect precisely this same racial and ethnic mix? And must each class also be balanced in the same way? Should the teachers in the schools also reflect racial and ethnic balances representative of the population as a whole? Pro-civil-rights groups often have answers to these questions different from those who have not worked for years in the effort to attain racial justice.

Some judges demanded immediate action, almost perfect racial balance of students and faculty, and classes inside the school that largely reflected the same balance. Others allowed a period of several years for gradual compliance and handed down less rigid guidelines with respect to percentages of black, white, and Hispanic students.

Along with others I watched the phenomenon of "white flight," in which desegregation court orders led to the massive movement of white families to the suburbs or enrollment in private schools to escape the impact of court-ordered busing of schoolchildren. In communities where this was not a problem, community leaders worked cooperatively with the courts because they knew that the actions taken were both necessary and reasonable.

Some federal judges took over many aspects of school management. In the city of Boston, for example, the court controlled almost all personnel actions; and it became involved in other actions that limited the powers of the school committee and superintendent of schools. Public reaction to such federal intervention was related to the perceptions that locally elected officials had been pushed aside and their schools were no longer under the control of those whom the public had elected.

On the other hand, federal officials had to be firm in enforcing the civil rights laws. Some local and state officials did try to subvert the intent of the laws enacted to protect the rights of minorities, and there was a need to be decisive.

In my approach to enforcement action taken by our Office of Civil Rights I favored moderation, low-profile discussion, and avoidance of confrontation if we could attain results without delay or denial of the rights of the plaintiffs. But this approach did not always work, and then we had to be more assertive with state and local officials. I had an aversion to the posturing that highlighted bold new initiatives in an effort to show that we had indeed "come here to make a difference." Some school desegregation busing plans were not working. A significant number had also resulted in even more segregation because of "white flight." These needed to be modified. But it was equally important to avoid sending out a signal that we opposed all desegregation plans, for many of them had yielded remarkable results.

In these debates with the Department of Justice and White House staff people, I had much to say about equal opportunity, the meaning of justice, civic morality, and "equal protection under the law." Despite supportive comments I had heard several times in meetings with the president, I never received any encouragement from others in the White House or from those in the Department of Justice to support enforcement of civil rights laws.

The ideals of our country demand this, just as they demand justice and equal protection under the law. And of all the services provided by government, educational opportunity must be administered in a manner that is evenhanded and nondiscriminatory. Knowing how free public schools and low-cost colleges had provided my ticket through the doorway to a better life, I have always felt a special aversion toward any person, group, or idea that obstructs or denies the opportunity to become educated.

Since I had heard Ronald Reagan speak out convincingly against all forms of discrimination, I felt that my own dedication to enforcement of the civil rights laws as they applied to education would have the full support of the president. But the reinterpretation of these statutes by some of the senior officers in his administration was alarming, and so was the evidence of apparent bias among mid-level right-wing staffers in the White House and at OMB.

I was shocked to hear their sick humor and racist clichés. For example, when the bill to establish a national holiday to honor Martin Luther King, Jr., was before the president for his signature or veto, these bigots referred to Dr. King as "Martin Lucifer Coon! Ha ha! We'll soon be able to celebrate Martin Lucifer Coon's birthday."

They delighted in making other slurs. Arabs were called "sand niggers." They referred to Title IX as "the lesbian's bill of rights." The former insult was usually heard in the context of State Department issues in the Middle East and the latter in discussions related to our struggles with the Justice Department over the law that ensures equal rights of women in schools and colleges.

Many of these people felt that Title IX was enacted to pacify masculine women who wanted women's athletic programs in schools and colleges. Such remarks ignore the fact that women have for years been denied equal opportunity in many important programs in school and college curricula such as law, medicine, engineering and mechanical and industrial fields. Discrimination on the basis of gender extended much deeper than lack of equal opportunity in athletic programs.

Since the regulations for Title IX had been written under the supervision, and with the active participation, of Caspar Weinberger when he was secretary of HEW, it was especially ironic to hear the allegations that the rules had been written by fuzzy-brained liberals. Title IX, like other titles in federal statutes, was a section of law commonly used by lawyers drafting language for Congress to enact, and this title simply extended the prohibition on the basis of race to include the same prohibition on the basis of sex.

I do not mean to imply that these scurrilous remarks were common utterances in the rooms and corridors of the White House and the Old Executive Office Building, but I heard them when issues related to civil rights enforcement weighed heavily on my mind so it seemed obvious they were said for my benefit, since they often accompanied sardonic references to "Comrade Bell."

A significant responsibility of the Office of Civil Rights (OCR) of the U.S. Department of Education is to investigate complaints from citizens who feel that their rights have been violated by actions taken by officers representing schools and colleges. This burden was formerly placed on the Department of Health, Education, and Welfare, and the responsibility was transferred to ED when it was created.

The enforcement of civil rights laws carries with it much emotion, thoughtful debate over interpretations of these laws, and verbal and legal combat from time to time over compliance of schools and colleges. The intensity and emotion had been growing since the Supreme Court ordered desegregation of schools that had been historically segregated by state law.

In the fall of 1970, a massive move to integrate many school systems in the Southern states took place. I was caught up unwittingly in this difficult but necessary action. I had just arrived in Washington for my first tour of federal service as deputy commissioner in the U.S. Office of Education when President Nixon fired my boss, U.S. Commissioner of Education James Allen.

I was asked by HEW Secretary Elliot Richardson to serve as acting commissioner of education pending the appointment and Senate confirmation of a new commissioner. This assignment, originally intended to be of very short duration, lasted for almost seven months. President Nixon appointed Sidney P. Marland, Jr., to succeed Jim Allen, but because Sid had recently been embroiled in a struggle with the teachers' union in Pittsburgh where he had served as superintendent of schools, the political weight of organized labor came down in opposition to Senate confirmation of his appointment. This resulted in a long period of hearings, delays, and further hearings, so while the controversy was being resolved, I had the full burden of the U.S. Office of Education on my back. This responsibility carried with it the additional job of running the U.S. Office of Education while my future boss, Sid Marland, looked on from a side office. To me, it seemed a bit like having your mother-in-law with you on your honeymoon. I did not relish the added surveillance.

In the U.S. Office of Education, we were required to assist the many federal courts in helping the judges draw up proposed new attendance boundaries for schools so that students would no longer be segregated by race. We also had to advise the courts on transportation matters as new bus routes were planned. And we worked with the courts on the reassignment of faculty and administration so that the racial mix of teachers and principals in the schools would be reasonably representative of the population. As experienced educators worked at these complex tasks, they were supervised and directed by their chief, the U.S. commissioner of education. These duties were a large part of my total responsibilities as acting commissioner during this crucial time.

I was ill prepared for the duties thrust upon me by Jim Allen's abrupt removal and only marginally aware of the impending struggle of the Southern states to integrate all their schools. Furthermore, I did not realize the depth of the emotion felt by those opposed to having their children sit in classrooms next to black children or having their children taught by a black teacher.

Being a member of the Mormon church in 1970 carried its own emotional impact in the eyes of black leaders. Although the church's position subsequently changed, at the time I moved into the commissioner's office in 1970 it permitted blacks to hold membership but did not allow black males to be ordained in the priesthood. In the minds of many blacks, this doctrine was offensive and a standing insult.

When word circulated among civil rights leaders that President Nixon had fired his commissioner of education and placed a Mormon in his position, the reaction against me was intense. During my seven months as acting commissioner civil rights leaders labeled me a racist because of my religion.

They could not have been more wrong. It is not enough to have knowledge of some things through cognition alone. One must acquire some essential understandings about compassion and justice in a deeper, more lasting way. It must be gut-level knowing. This level of commitment is acquired only through living what you learn. You then come to know what you know because your experiences in life stamp it deep within you. This level of learning is more meaningful than that acquired only through the intellect.

I will never know what it is like to endure prejudice because of belonging to a minority. I will not know it as the Jews know discrimination. I will never feel the stigma experienced by many Mexican Americans in the United States. How could one born into the majority ever know what it is like to receive unfair and demeaning treatment for no other reason than that one's skin is dark, one's heritage is demeaned, or one's religion is the target of age-old hatred?

But I came to my understanding of the rightness of the civil rights laws and the despicable wrongness of discrimination because I lived it to some extent.

In my small hometown we were the poor people to be pitied. Because of this, we were to be watched. In the minds of many, if you were a recipient of welfare or community giving, you were automatically different—certainly not very bright or well informed or as energetic and sophisticated as ordinary people.

When I was in elementary school the poor were given free dental exams. The dentist let me know that I was a different class of patient. I left his office feeling ashamed that I could not pay him. He took pains to see that I felt that way.

When I went grocery shopping for my mother I heard the local grocer comment about what were proper and improper expenditures for a widow and her children. Going back, some ladies would interrogate me about the contents of my grocery bag. I started to creep up the alley with my meager sack of groceries.

In Lava Hot Springs the management of the movie theater advertised by delivering handbills to the doorsteps of people's homes. A small boy could earn free admission to a movie by "peddling bills." On Mondays and Thursdays after school the first four boys to arrive at the movie theater office gained this right. If you wanted to compete for this privilege you had to be a good long-distance sprinter from school to the "show house."

When I became big enough to compete, I saw my first motion picture. It was a marvel to behold, but as I left a neighbor chastised me for wasting money.

"Terrel, your family can't afford to go to the movies," she said. "We all worry about you and try to help your family. Now, don't let me see you in here again."

The Bell family wore a stigmatizing label in Lava Hot Springs—the presumption of inferiority.

The big difference for me, of course, was that I was able to grow up and turn my life around. But in the eyes of the race-hating beholder, if I had been born black I would for all my years have been black first and a human being second.

I cannot think of any part of our nation's history that is more shameful than those years when discrimination was rampant.

ED's problems with the Department of Justice emerged from differences in reading and interpreting the words in the laws that both departments were required to enforce. In ED, we read the law from the perspective of educators who had worked in schools and colleges and understood admission, placement, and promotion procedures. We read the law broadly to assure equal educational opportunity. Justice lawyers were reading to find ways to "get the government off the backs of the people."

The words in Title VI of the Civil Rights Act of 1964 and words taken from this title and inserted by Congress in Title IX of the Education Amendments of 1972 were the source of disagreement between ED and Justice. This is the language from Title IX that prohibits sex discrimination:

No person in the United States shall, on the basis of sex, be excluded from participation in, be denied the benefits of, or be subjected to discrimination under any program or activity receiving federal financial assistance.

The disagreement centered on the words, "any program or activity receiving federal financial assistance." This same language had been used in the Civil Rights Act that was passed in 1964. The education community, the federal agencies responsible for enforcement, and the federal courts had all interpreted both the entire educational program and all the extracurricular activities of the school systems or colleges to be included within the meaning of these words. For almost two decades we had administered these laws with this broad inclusive intent.

The Department of Justice found encouragement to narrow the meaning of the words "program or activity" when a federal court in Virginia handed down a decision in *The University of Richmond* v. *Bell*. At issue in the case was alleged violation of Title IX at this institution. Women from the university had filed a complaint that they had been denied opportunity in athletics. The federal judge concluded that our Office of Civil Rights had no right to investigate the complaint because the athletic program or activity at the university did not receive federal financial assistance. It was acknowledged that the university received federal funding, but the court found that none of these funds went to the athletic program, so the federal statute prohibiting discrimination on the basis of sex did not apply to that specific program. Since the athletic department did not receive federal funds, it was free to discriminate against women.

When ED was involved in litigation over civil rights enforcement, we were required to use Department of Justice lawyers despite the fact that we had over sixty lawyers working for us. As we discussed the position to be taken in these cases, our Justice lawyers usually took the position that would narrow and limit enforcement authority. *The University of Richmond* v. *Bell* was a classic example of this, but there were many others.

All this activity in the federal courts made it apparent that we would soon have a major case before the United States Supreme Court. With the exception of a few small private institutions, there was broad acceptance and support of the civil rights laws to protect minorities, women, and the handicapped from discrimination. I could see no reason to come forth with a new interpretation of these laws. It would cause strife and bitterness among those currently enjoying the protection of the civil rights laws. With each new interpretation I became more and more apprehensive.

In all my contacts with Assistant Attorney General Reynolds I had the impression that his intent was to find gaps in the law through which he could avoid taking what I thought was necessary and desirable enforcement action. Brad Reynolds never agreed with my interpretation of his intent, but I was convinced that his actions were harmful to the course of equal opportunity in education.

We had, for years, considered an institution or school district obligated to comply with all the civil rights statutes if it received any federal financial assistance. This was widely known: If you take federal money you must comply. If you receive no federal funds you need not. It was as simple as that. That was the way we all read the law prior to Brad Reynolds' creative interpretations. The entire education community accepted this simple understanding as the law of the land.

Some colleges refused all federal funds because they were independent and private institutions and wanted passionately to be free from, any federal reporting, accountability, and control. Other private institutions eagerly applied for and gladly accepted federal funds with the full knowledge that they would have to show that they were in compliance with all civil rights rules.

But Brad Reynolds had another view of the law. He wanted to change the time-honored interpretation of civil rights coverage to narrow its application in all of education, both public and private. Civil rights coverage prior to Reynolds's interpretations did not cover schools or colleges that received no federal money. To do this, he looked at old language in the statute and read something much more restrictive into its wording.

The statute stated that "a program or activity" receiving federal financial assistance must be in full compliance with the civil rights requirements. Reynolds was convinced that "program" did not mean the overall educational program of the college or school district. To Reynolds the term was limited to the instruction offered in a particular department or discipline of the educational institution—the program of, say, the physics department rather than the total curriculum of the school or college. Thus, if there was a violation of equal rights in physics or athletics or any other division or activity of the institution, punitive action could be applied only to the offending department or division, and only if it received federal aid. The institution as a whole was not affected, and other constituents of the institution were free to discriminate as long as they were not receiving federal funds. The jurisdiction for civil rights enforcement was thereby narrowed dramatically. This restricted enforcement, which would apply to all schools and colleges, public and private, would remove protection against discrimination from minorities and others, and the impact would be far reaching.

At the same time that Reynolds sought to narrow the definition of "program or activity," he also broadened the definition of federal financial assistance by including indirect forms of federal aid, such as Pell grants to students, as aid to the institution.

This matter was contested in the courts under litigation that I inherited from my predecessors in a long and nasty dispute with Grove City College in Pennsylvania. The case became known as *Grove City* v. *Bell,* since I was the defendant in the suit filed by Grove City College. (It had been filed against my predecessors but following the usual practice, the defendant's name is changed when a government official leaves and a successor arrives.)

Grove City College is a private institution that refuses to accept federal money. It is fiercely independent and wants only one thing from the federal government: to be left alone. I wanted to respect that desire. The college did not to my knowledge discriminate on the basis of race, ethnic origin, or sex of its students. It accepted no federal funds, but some of the students attending the college did.

Grove City College admitted students who applied directly to the federal government for student aid under the Pell grant program. Here is how the program works: The low-income student applies for the grant. The grant is made by the federal government to the student to help him or her defray the cost of college attendance. In the case of Grove City College, the Pell grants were not even disbursed to the college for and on behalf of the student. Grove City had such a fierce desire to stay free of any kind of federal entanglement that it refused to accept federal money that was simply deposited with the college to disburse to the students at the time of registration.

Because of Grove City's refusal even to serve as a cashier or disbursing agent, the U.S. Department of Education, respecting the college's wishes, mailed government checks directly to the students. The students deposited the money in their private accounts and then used the funds for room and board, school clothing, books, supplies, tuition, or for any other education-related cost of attendance. Thus, they might or might not use the Pell grant funds to pay tuition to the college.

Given this, the aid in my judgment went to the students, and only indirectly to the college if it went there at all.

Nor was this my judgment alone. The same interpretation of Pell grant moneys had been held by enforcement authorities for a long time, and civil rights leaders as well as school and college administrators accepted it.

But though I took the position that the college received no financial assistance and was therefore not obligated to report to us, fill in forms, or sign assurances of compliance with civil rights laws, the Justice Department disagreed. Reynolds wanted to broaden civil rights coverage nationwide by interpreting the law to include *all* student aid as aid to the institution.

The vast impact of the Grove City litigation alarmed me. This change was not limited to a few private colleges that refused federal money; it would affect thousands of institutions. The Justice Department's stance required that any institution that admitted Pell grant recipients had to come under the surveillance of the civil rights laws. But because the jurisdiction applied only to that constituent of the institution that received the money, we would be forced to monitor and trace funds *within* each institution in order to identify the recipient unit or department. The tracing would be an administrative nightmare and make enforcement enormously complex.

When the proposed new interpretation came out of the Department of Justice, I protested vigorously. We had already stopped judicial overenforcement. Compulsory busing was being moderated to allow more reasonable alternatives such as establishing magnet schools and allowing a less rigid ratio of black and white enrollments. We were concentrating on what black parents wanted: an acceptably high quality of education for their children.

Women's equity under Title IX was now interpreted in a way that was acceptable to those monitoring women's rights and those governing the institutions. I could see no reason for a radical change in definitions and guidelines. All in all, the educational world was steadily adjusting to the more moderate position we had taken in the Department of Education.

When complaints were filed we tried to talk with the institution heads as well as the plaintiffs. We found that most college presidents and school superintendents were as committed to the civil rights laws as we were. Negotiation rather than confrontation was working well. It was not time for a major legal maneuver to torture the language of the law to mean something entirely different from what had been accepted over years of practice.

I wanted to avoid the game plan cooked up in the Justice Department. I used my right to bring matters of conflict between two cabinet officers to the Oval Office for a decision. I knew that Ronald Reagan would want to avoid the uproar of a pitched battle. I was confident that he was not aware of the far-reaching consequences of this proposal.

The entire position was, in my view, harmful to American education and potentially damaging to the rights of minorities who had fought against discrimination for all these years. It was a major issue. The view of the Reagan administration before the Supreme Court in *Grove City* v. *Bell* had to be clarified. We had to take a stand, and I believed the Brad Reynolds proposal would be a disaster.

There needed to be a White House review of the conflict of opinion that existed between Attorney General William French Smith and myself. I prepared myself for the day when we would meet in the Oval Office to explain our fundamental differences.

When the day came, I was informed that we would meet in Meese's office rather than in the Oval Office with the president. He was preoccupied with other pressing matters, so this squabble between Justice and ED was delegated to Ed Meese for mediation.

As I walked in the door to meet with Ed and Bill Smith, the greeting from Meese, although expressed as a joke, let me know that nothing had changed in the right-wing view of me. "Is that the hammer and sickle?" he asked as he pointed to my necktie.

Meese was wearing his usual tie with the profile of Adam Smith scattered over it. I looked down at mine. It had been a gift from De Paul University when I visited their campus. It had some small red figures, emblems of De Paul, and wrapped around my collar, it inevitably was suggestive to Ed of my supposed leanings. I thought it a sour joke.

I spelled out to Meese the consequences of the Justice Department position on the Grove City case. I went into detail in describing the consequences of such a radical change in interpretation of the law. But given the fact that I wasn't going to be able to talk to the president directly, and knowing Meese's affiliation with the people of the movement, I knew that mine was a lost cause. The hammer-and-sickle greeting before I ever sat down at the table let me know where I stood.

The administration prepared its case before the Supreme Court in the Grove City matter. The brief filed with the Court argued that Pell grants were, indeed, aid to Grove City College. But the pleading before the Court went on to state that the "program or activity" applied only to the student aid office and not to the entire institution. So, despite the administration's view that Grove City College received federal aid by admitting students who had received Pell grants, the entire institution was free to discriminate if it chose, except for the student aid office.

Following the meeting in Meese's office, I was not involved in any further deliberations in developing the administration's brief. From that time forward the government's case was presented, of course, by the Office of the Solicitor General.

Much to my surprise and disappointment, the Court handed down a decision that was almost fully in support of the Brad Reynolds position. The reaction to the Court's action was immediate and widespread. Civil rights groups expressed shock and dismay, while the conservatives greeted the news with jubilation.

Members of Congress were equally surprised at the Court's interpretation of the language they had used in enacting the civil rights laws. Many claimed that it was not their intent to restrict enforcement authority as the Court had done in *Grove City*. A proposed new law, the Civil Rights Restoration Act, was introduced, but conflicts between liberal and conservative views kept the legislation in committee. It was clear that new civil rights legislation would eventually be enacted, but the process would take several years.

This action of Justice in this matter was, in my view, mean-spirited. Bill Smith's complaint to me that he had come to Washington to make a difference and that I was obstructing his good intentions was just a harbinger of more Justice Department actions.

Ed Meese became Attorney General early in 1985, when William French Smith left at the conclusion of the President's first term. In a different setting, at Tulane University, he announced that Supreme Court rulings are not the final law of the land. Another U.S. Attorney General, Elliot Richardson, had a good explanation for this change of view. "Where you stand depends upon where you sit," he declared.

CHAPTER 10

"A Nation at Risk"

Although the president's popularity was high, the nation itself was not in happy shape in 1981. Inflation was at the double digit level, interest rates were high (the prime rate had risen above 20 percent), and unemployment was widespread, with youth, especially minority youth, very hard hit. America's prestige and influence abroad had declined, and the ransacking of our Teheran embassy and the taking of hostages left the country feeling angry and impotent. The national mood was one of self-doubt and helplessness, a mood reflected in polls, the media, and the fruitless search for scapegoats. There was more soul-searching, wringing of hands, and criticism than confidence in those solutions that were proposed, and the actions the government did take appeared ineffective.

It was in the context of this pervasive decline, and the widespread questions it raised about what was wrong with our government, our people, our labor force, our businesses, and our schools, that I was hearing constant complaints about education and its effectiveness.

Although many of the criticisms of education were valid, the general malaise of the country was reflected in the schools. We needed to regain our confidence in the future. This had to happen on many fronts, but it had to begin with our schools. It is well known that most of the unemployed are uneducated, and there is a strong link between productivity and skilled intelligence. If we were to become more competitive and increase the nation's productivity, education had a significant role to play.

I had traveled across the land in my work with the ten regional offices of our department, and I knew of the disquiet about the vanished American spirit, of industries in trouble. Why were so many people having so much difficulty finding jobs? It was because so many lacked the basic skills to be retrained. Where were we going to find the technically and scientifically informed people for an increasingly complex world of work? How should schools face up to new social realities that, like it or not, were going to be with us for a long time to come: broken homes and poverty, especially in our inner cities?

These had all played a part in our waning ability to exert our influence and generate respect abroad and confidence at home. Our loss of zest and drive and spirit would not be regained until we renewed and reformed our schools.

We needed some means of rallying the American people around their schools and colleges. Educators also needed to be shaken out of their complacency. More than two decades ago the Soviet Sputnik had spurred us into action to improve educational standards and performance. We needed an equally powerful spur today.

I wanted to stage an event that would jar the people into action on behalf of their educational system. Since I could not realistically plan on another Sputnik-type occurrence, I had to search for an alternative.

I began to think about asking the president to appoint a first-rate panel to study the problems of American education. The response from my colleagues was dubious; this would be very unlikely to provide a solution or lead to action. I was reminded by some of my best friends inside ED and out in the world of academe that panels and reports are often used as excuses for not taking action. When in doubt, do a survey of the problem, and this will buy time.

But I knew from past history that this need not be the consequence of a study if it resulted in a hard-hitting report that sounded a credible alarm with which intelligent people could identify. Back in 1910, for example, the Flexner report shook the medical profession to its roots, and utterly transformed medical education and the standards and procedures of practice. At the end of World War II a report to the president and the Congress on appalling conditions in war-ravaged Europe led to the massive rebuilding program of the Marshall Plan. Each of these reports of dreadful conditions jolted people into action.

I knew from all that I was hearing that the deep anxiety about the country's future in general and its education system in particular was creating a condition of receptivity for a tough, powerful, persuasive report on the condition of American education and recommendations for change.

A presidentially appointed commission would provide optimum conditions for success. Since the president's prestige was so great, I wanted to persuade senior White House staff to support my idea.

I hoped to get such a panel charged by the president himself to perform the task of appraising the condition of our schools and reporting to the nation on what should be done to give us a first-rate education system. But when I took this idea to the White House it was met with diffidence or scorn. People don't pay attention to federal reports, I was told. Federal commissions are so ineffective that they go unnoticed, I heard. Education is a local and state responsibility, was a common reaction. If the president appointed a national panel to study our schools' problems, it would imply that there is a significant federal role in education when we all know there is none, was another, along with, it might even lead to more federal legislation when what we want is to get rid of what we already have.

The trial balloons I floated over to the White House generated an equal lack of enthusiasm from the Baker and the Meese sides. Clearly, a formal proposal to get the president to appoint a national commission would be rejected out of hand. So I decided to appoint my own commission. A cabinet-level commission would not carry the prestige of a presidentially appointed panel, but it was apparently my only option. If the commission had any impact at all, it would seem worthwhile.

In the appointment of commissions and advisory bodies that are temporary and created for a special purpose, federal law requires that certain procedures be followed. A charter must be written specifying the life span of the panel and its responsibilities. Though I had the legal authority to appoint the commission, the Office of Management and Budget had to approve its creation. To meet the OMB requirement turned out to be no small task. We started the usual paper blizzard flowing over to the Old Executive Office Building where OMB makes its nest. (A few mid-level staffers at the White House also became involved.) My action to move ahead on the cabinet level after the idea of a presidential panel had been rebuffed was considered by some people at OMB and the White House as an act of insubordination. While they could not stop me, they could give my staff who had been assigned to the project plenty of harassment. This went on for several weeks.

Fortunately my very able special assistant, Mrs. Mary Jean LeTendre, was fully equal to the task of combating red tape and bureaucratic impediments. She knew how to fight, and she was a diplomat as well as a bright and effective scrapper. Each objective was achieved by tact or by wearing down the opposition. A charter establishing the commission for a period of eighteen months was finally written and approved on August 26, 1981.

Next came the task of appointing the members. The mid-level White House people got into this act too. Those who had nothing but derisive remarks to make about the charter we had prepared decided that if we *were* going to have a cabinet-level commission, it should have a conservative membership. This intent had to be turned around. I wanted a commission whose membership would command respect and be beyond reproach. It had to be balanced; I wanted liberals and conservatives, Republicans and Democrats, males and females, minorities, educators and noneducators. Most of all, the panel's words had to be powerfully convincing to the American people.

The process of clearing names and beating down the strategy to stack the commission with the "right people" took an inordinate length of time. But eventually we succeeded in appointing eighteen very distinguished Americans to the newly created National Commission on Excellence in Education. (NCEE). There was not a single member who did not have my approval and full confidence that he or she would be effective.

A major obligation was to insure that we had adequate leadership. From the outset I knew that I must have David Pierpont Gardner, president of the University of Utah, as the chairman. I had worked with David during the years that I served as Utah commissioner of higher education, and he had all the qualities we needed to chair the commission and guide its work. He is a brilliant, articulate, personable man. He would be strong. He would not be overpowered by anyone in the federal government nor would he tolerate any interference with the work of his commission.

There were strong rumors that David Gardner was about to become the next president of the University of California. Since it was his native state, I was not surprised when he was appointed to this post. Despite his new responsibilities as chief executive officer of the nation's largest university system, he continued in his role on the commission.

David Gardner's success in carrying out the responsibility we had placed on him would be contingent on his having the necessary support and talent needed to do the research and carry out staff backup to the commission. I assigned this to our embattled research arm, the National Institute of Education.

Dr. Milton Goldberg, a senior staff associate at NIE, became the executive director of NCEE and met with Gardner to discuss the work of NIE staff in gathering data and giving other support to the commission. The chemistry between the two men was good from the start. Yvonne Larsen, who had just completed a term as president of the Board of Education of the San Diego Schools, was vice-chairperson. Other members included Dr. William O. Baker, a distinguished scientist and past president of Bell Telephone Laboratories; Dr. Bartlett Giamatti, president of Yale University; and Dr. Norman Francis, president of Xavier University in New Orleans and a distinguished black scholar.

Dr. Shirley Gordon, president of Highline Community College in the Seattle area, brought us the valuable perspectives of the community college and the Pacific Northwest. A Midwest orientation was provided by Robert Haderlein, a Kansas dentist who was president of the National School Boards Association. Dr. Francisco Sanchez, superintendent of schools in Albuquerque, was knowledgeable about the education needs of the growing Hispanic population. Insight derived from experience as both a governor and a lawmaker was provided by Albert Quie, who had been a member of the House of Representatives for many years before becoming governor of Minnesota.

Jay Sommer, the national 1981 Teacher of the Year, had invaluable knowledge of elementary and secondary schools; and Emeral Crosby, an outstanding black high school principal in Detroit, contributed greatly to the commission's understanding of inner city problems and realities. Richard Wallace, principal of a private Lutheran high school, was well informed about private school education, a sector of growing importance. Charles A. Foster, Jr., who had served as CEO of the California-based Foundation for the Teaching of Economics, was an articulate spokesman for disciplined teaching of basic skills, as well as education in economics.

Knowledge of state-level educational administration was contributed by Dr. Anne Campbell, who was commissioner of education in Nebraska. State boards of education have been occupying an increasingly important policy-making role, and Mrs. Margaret Marston of the Virginia State Board of Education represented that arm of the system. The parental viewpoint was contributed by Mrs. Annette Kirk. Two notable scientists, Dr. Gerald Holton of Harvard and Dr. Glenn Seaborg, a University of California Nobel laureate, completed our eighteen-member panel.

It had talent, range, and diversity, and I was delighted by the members' willingness to serve; busy people all, it was a measure of their commitment to the urgency of the problem. I was also a touch apprehensive. Each was strong willed and independent as well as rich in insight and experience, and even given Gardner's leadership skills, how realistic was it to expect that they would be able to reach a consensus?

Immediately after the commission was established, I asked Gardner to get the group together for orientation and clarification of procedures. There was much work to do, and the potential for drifting away from the central objectives prompted me to seek the best possible beginning.

At the first meeting the commission expressed concern about whether it would have total autonomy to do its work. There was no question about this. I had promised Gardner there would be no interference of any kind. Had I not done so, he would not have assumed the chairmanship.

I also promised the full resources of the Department of Education in support of the commission. I committed ED to the budget, the staff support, and full access to all data, computer assistance, and other needs. We had a vast amount of data in the U.S. Department of Education, but it had never been sifted, analyzed, and summarized in the coherent way that I hoped this panel would do. There were gaps in our data, and there were many new initiatives being taken each year. We wanted the commission to make a searching appraisal of these.

The commission members then asked the kind of questions that were at the root of White House staff reluctance to have a presidentially appointed commission. They wanted to know if I believed that the report they would release in eighteen months would make a difference—would make a significant contribution to the advancement of education.

"It will if you do your work and if it is of the highest quality," I replied. "You need unity in your conclusions if you can possibly attain it."

And what would happen after the report was released? What would the U.S. Department of Education and the Reagan administration do with it? David Gardner pressed this point aggressively and his colleagues joined him.

I promised that we would disseminate the results across the nation, through a series of dissemination conferences at which the report would be distributed and discussions held with those empowered to implement changes in education. These were, of course, the governors, state legislators, state education agencies, local school boards, administrators, teachers, and parents. We would strive to reach them all. This would be a top priority of my department immediately after the report was released. I could do no more than promise I would do all I could to get the president involved in the follow-up activities when the commission's study was released.

The press came to the commission's first meeting, and my commitments were reported to the public. I was on the record now. There could be no backing down on what had been agreed to. This satisfied the commission members, and they took up the challenge.

The commission report was due in March of 1983. They didn't make it. The members were hung up on several issues, and I was not at all surprised. Given this group of independent thinkers with such diverse backgrounds, I half expected a minority report.

But David Gardner wouldn't have this. He wanted his commission members to stand behind their report without any dissent.

During the eighteen-month period of the commission's deliberations, I had met with them several times, but always for the purpose of talking procedure and their support needs. I did not suggest or even hint at what I thought the commission's recommendations should be.

The commission conducted hearings in various parts of the country, and members of my immediate office staff attended many of them. My special assistant, Sharon Schonhout, for example, was assigned to cover the hearings in areas where there was a heavy Hispanic population. Despite being born and educated in Brooklyn, Sharon speaks fluent Spanish and has excellent rapport with Hispanics. She was the logical choice to gather reactions from people in the Southwest. Mary Jean LeTendre carried out the day-to-day liaison between my office and the commission and attended several hearings on my behalf. My chief of staff, Tom Anderson, was also active in providing assistance, encouragement, and resources needed by the commission. With the help of these three able colleagues, we looked after the needs of the commission but kept out of the deliberations. Had we at any time tried to influence the findings or recommendations, the members would have put us back in our place in an instant.

From their first session until the final release of their report, I was impressed with the professionalism and objectivity of their work. In a climate that encouraged freedom of expression, criticism, and debate, David Gardner pressed relentlessly to keep his colleagues from straying away from their charter. The full talents of all the members were thus utilized. There was intelligent intensity in their work, and I knew we would have a stimulating and thought-provoking report even if we had to settle for some minority views.

The commission not only held hearings to gather testimony from both experts and ordinary citizens, it also solicited papers to be written on topics of major concern. These were commissioned from many informed individuals who had outstanding credentials and had been recognized as authorities in their fields. These papers treated items of current concern such as the education and certification of teachers, the nature of academic work contained in the elementary and secondary schools, and the accreditation standards of schools.

The work of the commission was thorough, systematic, and intensive. They had a deadline to meet. They used their time wisely, and they pursued their objectives relentlessly.

As the charter deadline approached, I realized that before many months, we would be involved in the 1984 election campaign. I wanted the report out and the dissemination conferences completed before the election season descended on us. Given our appallingly prolonged election campaigns, extended a few more days or weeks every four years, I knew we could tolerate no delay.

But postponement was what David Gardner asked for. He called me early in February of 1983 to tell me that the commission needed another month. The president had agreed to receive the report and respond to its recommendations in a carefully planned public release, and we had scheduled the release of the report at the White House for late March. Since the commission was looked upon with scorn by the rightists who populated many White House offices, I felt it was a stroke of luck to have gotten on the president's calendar at all. If we tried to reschedule, I was far from sanguine about the prospect of presidential participation, and without the president, we would lose the attention of the huge White House press corps. We needed network TV, the wire services, and the giants among the nation's newspapers to cover this event if we were to get our message out. Everything we hoped to attain rested on this, and it in turn rested on the president's presence.

"Dave, we can't get the president. At least, I don't think we can if we put this off another month," I protested.

"We need [the] unanimous support of all commission members [for] every aspect of the report," David replied. "I can get the four or five who are in disagreement to join the majority, but it will take me more time to mediate the differences."

"Let's go with it as it is," I said. "We won't get all eighteen of you to agree unanimously on anything."

"I believe I can. I need some time for discussion, and then one more plenary session."

Gardner was so firm that I knew I couldn't pressure him anymore. He was right in what he wanted to do, though I wondered if he fully understood the climate in which we were working. I agreed that we would try for a release in late April, but we would keep the specific date flexible to accommodate the president's calendar.

I put the phone down with a groan so loud that my colleagues came in to see if I had suffered a heart attack or something worse.

"We've got to postpone the release," I announced with my head in my hands.

"I knew it!" Mary Jean replied. "The commission's members are pushing so hard for their viewpoints that there hasn't been time to get them to reach a consensus."

"They'll never get together. Not all of them," I said. "We'll be in the same position a month later. I tried too hard to get diversity and prestige on that panel. It serves me right. I picked too many independent thinkers."

"Let them work it out," Tom Anderson advised. "We can still get the president. We can call the White House, but before we do, let's see what we can learn about his late-April calendar."

Mary Jean did the detective work, and the calendar seemed to be okay for the last ten days of the month. But the possibility that unexpected events would preempt a commitment to us was always present.

With this information, I called White House Chief Jim Baker to plead my case for a delay. He was very understanding and sympathetic. He and Cabinet Affairs Director Craig Fuller seemed to appreciate the significance of the commission's work. This support was the only reason I had received any attention from the president in the first place.

Jim Baker asked for an early draft of the report so the president could be briefed. I explained that we were still several weeks away from seeing a first draft ourselves, but I promised a copy as soon as possible.

A few days later he called with a commitment of April 26 on the president's calendar. I was elated. We agreed to make our release on that date. Would the commission members still be hung up? On that note, I called Dave Gardner to tell him the good news.

"How are you coming?" I asked.

"We're coming along." he replied a bit evasively.

"I can't delay again," I warned.

"Don't worry, Ted. We'll make it."

And they did. The report was indeed adopted by unanimous action of all the members of the commission. David Gardner had performed a miracle.

The next worry was to get the Government Printing Office to meet our very tight time schedule. Dr. Milton Goldberg, the commission's executive director, battled through the red tape, and the printing process was under way. We would have a report in hand, and it would have the full support of the commission members. I was ready for some good news and the taste of success.

It was time for me to read the draft of the report that had gone to the printer. I had kept my word on not asking to see the report prior to its adoption by the commission. I didn't know what the findings would be or what proposals would be made to improve the nation's schools. I was, of course, deeply concerned about the impact the report would have on the president, my colleagues in the cabinet, and my friends and critics at the White House. Like that of the Republicans' symbolic elephant, the report's gestation period had been over eighteen months. Not many were concerned about the delivery, and others were certain we would strain mightily and give birth to a miserably insignificant mouse.

My first reading of the report left me surprised, elated, and apprehensive all at the same time. I didn't doubt that the report would be an attention getter. But I wondered how the education community would react to it. The typewritten pages in my hands could bring its wrath down on us. It was hard hitting. It was critical. It was a warning as well as an indictment of all of us—parents, educators, political leaders, taxpayers, and students.

Its title was explosive too: *A Nation at Risk: The Imperative for Educational Reform.* The cover also bore the words "An Open Letter to the American People." At the bottom it declared that it was "A Report to the Nation and to the Secretary of Education by the National Commission on Excellence in Education."

Inside the front cover was a transmittal letter addressed to the secretary of education. It admonished me to disseminate the findings and recommendations and summarized the commission's convictions:

> Our purpose has been to help define the problems afflicting American education and to provide solutions, not search for scapegoats. We addressed the main issues as we saw them, but have not attempted to treat the subordinate matters in any detail. We were forthright in our discussion and have been candid in our report regarding both the strengths and weaknesses of American education.
>
> The Commission deeply believes that the problems we have discerned in American education can be both understood and corrected if the people of our country, together with those who have public responsibility in the matter, care enough and are courageous enough to do what is required.

And the opening pages were just as trenchant:

> Our Nation is at risk. Our once unchallenged preeminence in commerce, industry, science, and technological innovation is being overtaken by competitors throughout the world. This report is concerned with only one of the many causes and dimensions of the problem, but it is the one that undergirds American prosperity, security, and civility. We report to the American people that while we can take justifiable pride in what our schools and colleges have historically accomplished and contributed to the United States and the well-being of its people, the educational foundations of our society are presently being eroded by a rising tide of mediocrity that threatens

our very future as a Nation and a people. What was unimaginable a generation ago has begun to occur—others are matching and surpassing our educational attainments.

If an unfriendly foreign power had attempted to impose on America the mediocre educational performance that exists today, we might well have viewed it as an act of war. As it stands, we have allowed this to happen to ourselves. We have even squandered the gains in student achievement made in the wake of the Sputnik challenge. Moreover, we have dismantled essential support systems which helped make those gains possible. We have, in effect, been committing an act of unthinking, unilateral educational disarmament.

Our society and its educational institutions seem to have lost sight of the basic purposes of schooling, and of the high expectations and disciplined effort needed to attain them. This report, the result of 18 months of study, seeks to generate reform of our educational system in fundamental ways and to renew the Nation's commitment to schools and colleges of high quality throughout the length and breadth of our land.

That we have compromised this commitment is, upon reflection, hardly surprising, given the multitude of often conflicting demands we have placed on our nation's schools and colleges. They are routinely called on to provide solutions to personal, social, and political problems that the home and other institutions either will not or cannot resolve. We must understand that these demands on our schools and colleges often exact an educational cost as well as a financial one.

On the occasion of the Commission's first meeting, President Reagan noted the central importance of education in American life when he said: "Certainly there are few areas of American life as important to our society, to our people, and to our families as our schools and colleges." This report, therefore, is as much an open letter to the American people as it is a report to the Secretary of Education. We are confident that the American people, properly informed, will do what is right for their children and for the generations to come.

History is not kind to idlers. The time is long past when America's destiny was assured simply by an abundance of natural resources and inexhaustible human enthusiasm, and by our relative isolation from the malignant problems of older civilizations. The world is indeed one global village. We live among determined, well-educated, and strongly motivated competitors. We compete with them for international standing and markets, not only with products but also with the ideas of our laboratories and neighborhood workshops. America's position in the world may once have been reasonably secure with only a few exceptional well-trained men and women. It is no longer.

The risk is not only that the Japanese make automobiles more efficiently than Americans and have government subsidies for development and export.

It is not just that the South Koreans recently built the world's most efficient steel mill, or that American machine tools, once the pride of the world, are being displaced by German products. It is also that these developments signify a redistribution of trained capability throughout the globe. Knowledge, learning, information, and skilled intelligence are the new raw materials of international commerce and are today spreading throughout the world as vigorously as miracle drugs, synthetic fertilizers, and blue jeans did earlier. If only to keep and improve on the slim competitive edge we still retain in world markets, we must dedicate ourselves to the reform of our educational system for the benefit of all—old and young alike, affluent and poor, majority and minority. Learning is the indispensable investment required for success in the "information age" we are entering.

Our concern, however, goes well beyond matters such as industry and commerce. It also includes the intellectual, moral, and spiritual strengths of our people which knit together the very fabric of our society. The people of the United States need to know that individuals in our society who do not possess the levels of skill, literacy, and training essential to this new era will be effectively disenfranchised, not simply from the material rewards that accompany competent performance, but also from the chance to participate fully in our national life. A high level of shared education is essential to a free, democratic society and to the fostering of a common culture, especially in a country that prides itself on pluralism and individual freedom.

For our country to function, citizens must be able to reach some common understanding on complex issues, often on short notice and on the basis of conflicting or incomplete evidence. Education helps form these common understandings, a point Thomas Jefferson made long ago in his justly famous dictum:

> I know no safe depository of the ultimate powers of the society but the people themselves; and if we think them not enlightened enough to exercise their control with a wholesome discretion, the remedy is not to take it from them but to inform their discretion.

Part of what is at risk is the promise first made on this continent: All, regardless of race or class or economic status, are entitled to a fair chance and to the tools for developing their individual powers of mind and spirit to the utmost. This promise means that all children by virtue of their own efforts, competently guided, can hope to attain the mature and informed judgment needed to secure gainful employment, and to manage their own lives, thereby serving not only their own interests but also the progress of society itself.

The report went on to cite the specifics of the risk, among them twenty-three-million illiterates, a steady decline in academic achievement, striking increases in college students taking remedial mathematics, a dramatic decline in science achievement, and writing skills such that only one-fifth of the nation's seventeen-year-olds could write a persuasive essay.

As I hurried through my draft copy, I realized that this was not a government report that would gather dust on the shelves. For one thing, it was only thirty-six pages long, not counting the appendix. It was concise, eloquent, and it had a profoundly important message.

The language reflected the penchant for clarity that was David Gardner's style in speaking as well as writing, and the content reflected the work of scholars who were practical as well as informed.

I had never seen so much substance in so brief a span. What would the reaction be? How would the press respond? Education administrators and teachers would almost certainly be angry. There were words of encouragement and recommendations for reform, but it was difficult to find a compliment on any page.

The report told the American people that the gap between the performance and the needs of American education was enormous. It was the product of neglect, misplaced priorities, and low standards. We are all to blame, it said. We are not productive. We have been losing our markets to well-educated and highly motivated competitors from abroad. We are squandering our most precious resource: human intelligence. We can't be ignorant and free. We can't help the American people to continue to enjoy the standard of living in the future that they have enjoyed in the past if we continue to spawn illiterates, lower standards and expectations, and neglect our teachers.

It was a cry for reform.

In a week the report would be released at the White House. I urged that it be kept in strict confidence so that leaks to the press would not dilute its impact or take the edge off the sharpness of its criticism. I knew there was concern there about what the report might say, for Ed Meese and his staff were afraid that the commission might propose a huge new federal spending program for schools. I had been advised in no uncertain terms that such a proposal from his administration would embarrass the president. I had answered that I did not know what the content would be. This response drew sharp remarks about my stewardship and failure to protect the president from criticism.

I was worried as usual about distancing. The tone as well as the content would raise eyebrows and hackles, and when controversy arises and trouble may be brewing is precisely when the White House separates itself from the offending federal department or agency. It has the effect of saying: This situation is entirely and independently the product of those inept crazies over in the department, so don't associate that mess with us.

The day after I first read it, I transmitted *A Nation at Risk* to President Reagan. How would he react? Would he read it or merely react to the briefing of his staff? Since it was so concise, I hoped he would have the time to read it. To grasp its full meaning, he should read every word and not just take it secondhand from a paraphraser's interpretation.

The report called for greater financial support for schools and for more competitive salaries for teachers. But it did not fix the level— federal, state, or local—from which this funding should come. The report also called for teachers' salaries to be performance based as well as professionally competitive. This would please the president, who was a longtime advocate of merit pay. Much of the report was in harmony with his recommendations to Congress in his State of the Union message of a few weeks before. It emphasized the place of technology, scientific research, and mathematics in today's world of work, commerce, and manufacturing.

Overall, I felt that he could support its findings and recommendations while rejecting massive federal spending.

A few hours after its transmittal I began to receive commendations for the draft of *A Nation at Risk* that was circulating at the White House. Later I heard from Craig Fuller that the president had read the full report and was very pleased with it. I put the phone down and shouted "Hooray!" I had needed his endorsement, and I had it.

Two days before the scheduled release of *A Nation at Risk,* we worked out the final arrangements for launching our campaign for educa- tion reform. The president would meet the members of the commission in the Oval Office to express his appreciation. Vice President Bush, Ed Meese, and Craig Fuller would also be there. We would present the president with an official copy in a brief ceremony.

Since the East Room of the White House was committed for this day, it was agreed that we would hold the release ceremony in the State Dining Room. The full press corps, including all the TV commenta- tors and their cameramen, would be invited. A cross section of the leadership structure of American education had been invited previously. They would comprise the audience that would receive copies of the report and a summary of the work of the commission's work from David Gardner. I was to be master of ceremonies, and I would greet the president, present him with the report, and introduce him to our guests.

During these preparations I wondered about the reticence of the ultraconservatives who had been so persistently my nemesis over the

months. Where were they? Here we were releasing a big study on education. Here was the president about to speak out on the schools, teachers,
and the educational establishment. For those who wanted a constitutional
separation between school and state to parallel the well known separation
between church and state, this action of their hero, Ronald Reagan,
would be a bit much. This was not the way to let Reagan be Reagan.
You don't feature the secretary of education in a big show-and-tell party
at the White House led by the president and then renew your determination
to abolish Department 13.

Where were these people? Were they not aware of what was about
to happen? Had they given up?

Late on the day before the April 26 release date, I received evidence
that they were still alive and feisty.

I had a call from my usual informant in the Baker camp.

"Doctor Bell," she began, "I hate to tell you this, but I just saw
a draft of the president's remarks for tomorrow. It misses the points of
your report. In fact, it ignores the report."

"What do you mean?" I asked. "How could it ignore the report?
The purpose of the meeting is for its release."

"Well, it doesn't exactly ignore the report, but it spends a lot of
time on school prayer, tuition tax credits, the value of private schools,
and the evils of the NEA."

"We'll get that changed," I said.

"I doubt it. These remarks were put in at the insistence of Ed Meese."

I was stunned.

"A group went in to see Ed. They were led by your 'friend,' Ken
Cribb," she said sardonically. "Ken's the one who hit Ed hard on
this. He argued that you can't have the president speaking on education
before an audience of this size and not hit tuition tax credits and school
prayer."

"I'll call Jim Baker in the morning," I said.

"I doubt if he'll want to fight Ed on this. It's not that big a deal."

"The report's emphasis will be obscured," I said. "The press reports
will be on what the president said and not on our report. We don't
have a single word on school prayer and tuition tax credits."

"Jim can't fight over every little thing," she said. "But you better
get him today, tomorrow may be too late."

I hung up in dismay. I had been right to wonder why everything
was moving along so smoothly. Our neighborly adversaries in the West
Wing wanted to use the occasion for more missionary work, seeking
converts to their agenda. Though the audience would not be large, its

eminence and the potential for media response made it worth their efforts.

I put in a call immediately for Jim Baker. He called back in a matter of minutes. I always wondered why the busiest man in the White House was the promptest in returning his phone calls.

"Jim, I just learned that the draft of the president's remarks tomorrow dwell more on tuition tax credits and school prayer than on our report."

"I haven't seen any draft yet," he said. "Are you sure about that?"

"I'm fairly certain," I said without revealing my source.

"I understand the president's concern for school prayer and tuition credits," I added, "but we don't treat those subjects one way or the other in this report. They're extraneous and irrelevant. I don't want the report's impact to be diluted by those two issues."

"I'll get back to you," Jim replied.

In a short time, he called to tell me that the issues were all settled. The offensive items would be out of the speech. The president would devote more time to the highlights of *A Nation at Risk*.

The next morning, just twenty minutes before the president was scheduled to appear in the State Dining Room, I heard on my car telephone that the prepared remarks had been changed again and the president would indeed be emphasizing school prayer legislation and tuition tax credits. I was en route to the White House and the last guests were being cleared at the gates as I got there. Whatever the president was to say, I had to live with it now.

The gathering in the State Dining Room was impressive. The leadership people from all the major education organizations were there, the women and men who could help us lead in school reform and renewal. Almost all of those asked had accepted our invitation.

Most impressive of all was the gathering of the news media. They were all on hand. The back of the room was filled with television cameras. Reporters with note pads and copies of *A Nation at Risk* had filled every available press seat. Had this meeting been at the Department of Education we would never had had such coverage.

We had special seating up front for the members of the commission. We had thirty minutes to brief the press and the distinguished educators in our audience before the President arrived. I introduced the commission members, made a few comments about their work and their report, and turned the podium over to David Gardner.

David spoke briefly on behalf of the commission. He described their hearings, the research, and the data-gathering process, and turned the microphone back to me.

It was time to present the president. I looked to the open door to the room on my right. He was not there. An aide signaled that it would be just a moment. I waited for a short time that seemed like an eternity. Still no president.

The audience began to squirm. All I could do was fill in the time. I talked about how the commission was formed. I discussed the significance of the report. I told about our plans for dissemination. Between sentences, I would glance over to see if we had a president. Still no Ronald Reagan.

A note was passed up that he had been delayed. Could I hold the audience for a time? I did my best. I talked about the need for the best leadership we could have for education. I looked over. Still no president.

It became obvious I was stalling, and the audience began to smile.

At long last, the president arrived. He bounded up onto the small platform. David Gardner and I greeted him. I presented him to the audience and to the huge press delegation and sat down.

The president fished into his pocket for the note cards he always used when speaking, apologized for his lateness, and then started on the remarks that had been prepared by his staff. It was almost identical to the speech that I had read and rejected. The words that I thought Jim Baker had gotten excised from the script came off those cards with the usual Reagan eloquence and style.

He did talk about the report. He hit teacher merit pay in particular. He praised the work of the commission. He mentioned other highlights of the report very briefly and emphasized the importance of education and how essential it was that the commission's recommendations be implemented.

Then he exhorted us on the need for students to be free to pray in school, telling that this was a fundamental right that must be restored. He followed this with the logic he had so effectively utilized in previous addresses on tuition tax credits. He described the need for choice. He emphasized the value of competition in education.

I have been a champion of private schools and colleges all my life. I had no objection to tuition tax credits for parents who sent their children to private schools. But the purpose of the meeting was to present the commission's report, and this was not the time or the proper setting for this issue any more than it was the proper setting in which to emphasize the issue of prayer.

To my relief, the audience knew this. They were glancing sideways and giving each other knowing looks.

As the president launched into that part of his speech that treated the prayer issue I looked over into the foyer just off the State Dining

Room to see Ken Cribb give a congratulatory gesture and victory sign to his fellow defenders of the right. Ed Meese was standing there with a big smile on his face.

The response to the publication of *A Nation at Risk* was overwhelming. Its impact by far exceeded my highest expectations. The extraneous material in the president's remarks was either ignored or referred to at the end of the press accounts as unrelated to the occasion. Its impact on the report's reception was almost zero. In fact, some newspaper cartoons made fun of the president's call for prayer and tuition tax credits.

Our press clipping service revealed that the commission's report was on the front page of all the major newspapers in every city—small, medium, and large—across the nation. Editorials appeared the next day. The news on the three major TV networks featured *A Nation at Risk*.

I was an instant celebrity. The next day I had invitations to appear on the highly visible early morning news shows. Requests came for me to appear the following Sunday on ''Meet the Press'' and ''Face the Nation.''

David Gardner and his colleagues on the commission were also in demand for appearances. Phone calls and letters poured in from across the country. We had hit a responsive chord. Education was on everyone's front burner.

Even David Stockman joined the chorus. The notes I scribbled on the face of a subsequent cabinet meeting agenda indicated that he gave the usual admonition to the cabinet to send in budgets for the next fiscal year that would drastically reduce expenditures. But he added an unprecedented concession: ''The sensitive issue of education is an exception, of course. We will want to keep out front on this. Other than that, stick to the targets I gave you.''

Stockman did not propose an increase in funds for the Department of Education's programs, but the huge cuts proposed to Congress in previous years were not mentioned when we worked with OMB on the next budget. What a difference! What a contrast were these priorities for spending!

The rush on copies of the report caused the U.S. Government Printing Office to go out of stock almost instantly, and it was behind on orders for months after publication date.

Newspapers printed the full text of *A Nation at Risk* in their Sunday editions. Syndicated columnists discussed aspects of the report. The follow-up on its various recommendations kept the small blue booklet before the public day after day.

Friends from my home in Salt Lake City sent me a copy of the Wednesday morning, April 27, 1983, *Salt Lake Tribune*. Its coverage was typical. Two banner headlines, at the top right and top left, heralded the message of *A Nation at Risk*.

The press highlighted the report's major message, quoting David Gardner at the presentations: "We're strategically vulnerable as a nation. How many missiles Russia has is less significant than this education situation."

Every item in the report came under national scrutiny. It charged that the condition of the teaching profession was poor. Our best teachers often left the profession after less than five years of service; the least qualified stayed on.

College students who were education majors preparing to teach had some of the lowest college entrance examination scores. Indeed, more than half of them scored in the bottom 25 percent. Additionally, half the newly employed math, science, and English teachers were not qualified to teach their subjects. Less than one-third of the high schools offered courses in physics that were taught by qualified teachers. (Points such as these were the reason I had tried to persuade the president to propose a new federally funded mathematics, science, and technology program.)

How could we build a great teaching profession from this new entry level talent of this caliber? How could we attract more capable teachers? The commission emphasized, "Salaries for the teaching profession should be increased and should be professionally competitive, market sensitive, and performance based. Salary, promotion, tenure, and retention decisions should be tied to an effective evaluation system that includes peer review so that superior teachers can be rewarded, average ones encouraged, and poor ones either improved or terminated."

I knew that this recommendation, if implemented, would make teaching a more respected and more attractive profession.

The commission was harshly critical of the overall quality of textbooks. This emphasis pleased me because I had long been convinced that our textbooks were not sufficiently challenging. It was no surprise that a study of textbook content revealed that a majority of the students were able to master about 80 percent of the contents of the subject matter in the texts before they ever opened them.

The textbook issue needed attention for reasons not mentioned in the study. The problems of "dumbing down" of textbooks are caused by the state adoption and selection processes and not by the publishers. Publishers in the school textbook field face some very thin and competitive markets. Investments in new textbooks are enormous, and the probabilities for profits are not high.

Two large states—Texas and California—dominate elementary and secondary school textbook choices because they decide which books their school systems will use statewide. The states appoint committees that review proposed texts and adopt those that meet their criteria. Readability criteria often call for vocabulary that is easy to master, for example, so students will not have to struggle unduly in reading science or social studies materials. Some textbook selection committees also seek nontechnical language in science books. Each year, as student academic competence has declined, the level of difficulty has been adjusted down accordingly.

Publishers must win the adoption contests in these large states or lose a big share of the total market. Since many states have no adoption procedure, those that do have even more power in influencing textbook content. Thus, the state committees' decisions influence education nationwide despite the fact that action is ostensibly taken only on behalf of the adopting states.

For nineteen consecutive years the nation's high school graduates distinguished themselves by scoring lower than their predecessor class in college entrance examinations. Standards and expectations had been reduced steadily in order to keep students in school. Nonetheless dropout and illiteracy rates had accelerated. Students were spending less time in school than they spent watching television. All these facts were thoroughly documented.

Perhaps the most telling criticism of all came from analysis of state-by-state high school graduation requirements. Thirty-five states required only one year of mathematics in high school. Thirty-six required only one year of science for a high school diploma. The study found that in many schools time spent learning how to drive a car or how to cook counted as much toward a high school diploma as time spent studying mathematics, English, biology, chemistry, or history.

Perhaps the commission's most prudent act was to define what it meant by *excellence* in education. Its definition accorded with the meaning we gave it in writing the commission's charter:

> We define "excellence" to mean several related things. At the level of the individual learner, it means performing on the boundary of individual ability in ways that test and push back personal limits, in school and in the work place. Excellence characterizes a school or college that sets high expectations and goals for all learners, then tries in every way possible to

help students reach them. Excellence characterizes a society that has adopted these policies, for it will then be prepared through the education and skill of its people to respond to the challenges of a rapidly changing world. Our Nation's people and its schools and colleges must be committed to achieving excellence in all these senses.

Advocates of minority, disadvantaged, and handicapped children criticized the report as "elitist," claiming that it addressed only the needs of the bright, the academically talented. But this criticism was not valid. The commission had made its position clear:

> We do not believe that a public commitment to excellence and educational reform must be made at the expense of a strong public commitment to the equitable treatment of our diverse population. The twin goals of equity and high-quality schooling have profound and practical meaning for our economy and society, and we cannot permit one to yield to the other either in principle or in practice. To do so would deny young people their chance to learn and live according to their aspirations and abilities. It also would lead to a generalized accommodation to mediocrity in our society on the one hand or the creation of an undemocratic elitism on the other.
>
> Our goal must be to develop the talents of all to their fullest. Attaining that goal requires that we expect and assist all students to work to the limits of their capabilities. We should expect schools to have genuinely high standards rather than minimum ones, and parents to support and encourage their children to make the most of their talents and abilities.

Utilizing these objectives, every student can attain excellence. Those least endowed are challenged to perform at their outer limits. These are *their* limits, not the limits of those who are academically powerful or of the near-genius level.

Thanks to the vice president, I had a unique opportunity to disseminate the commission's findings to an influential audience in the summer following the report's release in April 1983. We were vacationing in Maine with our twelve-year-old son Peter, and George and Barbara Bush invited us to visit them for a few days at their summer home in Kennebunkport. Peter won triumphant contests with two adult Bush sons on their electronic video game machine and then took on their father successfully. All of us, Bushes and Bells together, went for a demonic ride on the vice president's oceangoing speedboat. He was behind the wheel, and we were airborne half the time. The Secret Service and Coast Guard people tried to keep up with us in their security vessel but they never had a chance. Betty's sun hat flew off and disappeared into the cold Atlantic. Exhilarated—and awed by George Bush's seamanship—we came back to shore, where he offered her a choice of hats from his closet. She still wears this Maine memento, blazoned with the names Churchill Downs and Kentucky Derby.

On Sunday we all drove to church in the Vice President's huge bulletproof car, followed as always by the Secret Service. He had told us his eighty-three-year-old mother would be over to demand an explanation if we did not show up at services. We headed out to the road and up the hill, and on the way we passed his mother bicycling vigorously up the same hill toward the church. At Sunday dinner afterwards, we had the pleasure of discovering that her keen mind and acute sense of humor matched her vigor.

But the Vice President had an additional agenda for me. The nation's governors were holding their annual meeting in Portland, near the Bush home, and the Bushes had invited them all over for a lobster feast and clambake. It was a grand party, casual, delicious—and huge, since the governors brought their advance people, assistants, and security men. George Bush knew I would be eager to take advantage of the governors' presence, listen to their questions, friendly or critical, and push for implementation of *A Nation at Risk*.

I was indeed grateful for this forum, though it was often an uncomfortable one. Governor Mark White of Texas attacked the Reagan administration record on education. When Governors Richard Celeste of Ohio and William Clinton of Arkansas insisted that it was hardly fair for the administration to back a report admonishing the states for the decline in educational quality when the president continued to press for more budget cuts, I could hear the sense of their protests yet was committed to silence. It was my all-too-familiar dilemma, in which I had to defend the president's policies officially at the same time that I pushed for reform.

But there were positive responses as well, and these cheered me. Governors Richard Riley of South Carolina, Lamar Alexander of Tennessee, Robert Orr of Indiana, Bob Graham of Florida, Tom Kean of New Jersey, and Scott Matheson of Utah—who as chairman of the National Governors Association was in a particularly strategic position to bolster my efforts—were vigorous in support. And indeed, over the next three years many governors responded to the proposals in *A Nation at Risk* by pressing legislatures, school boards, educators, and the public to adopt tough new standards of academic excellence. In those states in which the greatest progress was made, the governors were in the forefront urging change and pushing for new revenues to fund improvements. I believe that the freewheeling discussions in Kennebunkport helped set the stage for many of these reforms.

The governors also delivered a valid criticism of the Department of Education that I acted on as quickly as possible when I got back to Washington. They said they had no information that told them where their states stood educationally in comparison to others. Lacking this, they were defenseless when their state superintendents and commissioners of education insisted that students in *their* state were above the national average in academic achievement. If you believed these top-level state school officers, just about every state in the country was above the national average! Though many of the seriously concerned governors knew this was far from true, there was little they could do without data to support their efforts for change.

As it turned out, putting together accurate assessments of each state's educational standing proved to be much more complex and controversial than I had anticipated. Gathering academic achievement test scores state by state turned out to be an utter impossibility. We had been funding a national assessment of educational progress program for several years, but the contracting organization did not have consistent data. Some states participated while others refused. Some states left it up to each local school district to respond to the assessment project. If its purpose was to provide state-by-state comparisons for the governors, this program was not a reliable source of information.

We finally decided to use college entrance examination scores, which were available on a state-by-state basis, and were based on two major standardized exams administered by two different national testing and evaluation companies. The scholastic aptitude test (SAT) was used in twenty-two states and the District of Columbia, and the American College Testing Program was widely used in twenty-eight states. These scores were aggregated into a statewide score each year. Colleges and universities used these examinations for student admission and placement decisions. Therefore, they did represent some measure of entering college students' readiness for college level work.

The test data have limitations, of course, since they do not take into account the performance of the many high school seniors, including those who do not plan to go on to college, who see no reason to take the exam. What is more, a higher percentage of high school graduates takes the test in some states than in others.

SAT and ACT scores are also criticized as measures of aptitude or ability rather than of academic accomplishment. But an item-by-item analysis of the college entrance examinations reveals that almost every single question relates to subject matter that is or should be taught in high school. Additionally, if colleges consider these tests to yield valuable information for admission and placement decisions on entry-level college students, the tests must also tell us how well the schools in the various states are preparing their students to do college-level work.

Since there were no other data more comprehensive, reliable, and nationwide in scope than these college entrance examination results, I decided to publish each state's scores and rank them state by state. But we also displayed the percentage of the state's high school graduates that took the exam and presented that figure alongside the state's scores and rankings. We included an explanation of the college entrance test rankings with these data and cautioned users not to jump to simplistic conclusions.

We showed other data on each state as well. We gave the percentage of the school age population of each state that lived in homes with incomes below the poverty level as determined by the Department of Commerce. We indicated the percentage of the states' student population that were minorities. We showed per capita income, teachers' salaries, and expenditures per child on a state-by-state basis.

It was also important to compare the student dropout rate on a state-by-state basis. States that had high dropout rates but high college entrance scores might be educating the best and neglecting those desperately in need of education. So we also ranked the states in their abilities to keep students in school through high school graduation.

After several months of hard work, we were ready to send to all fifty governors our rankings of the states from first to last. We printed a huge, extensively footnoted wall chart. Along with the chart we sent to each governor and each chief state school officer a comprehensive written explanation of the data. We discussed frankly the weak points as well as the strengths of our report.

We released the ranking of the states (simply called the "education wall chart" in some circles) at a press conference held in the Horace Mann Center at the Department of Education in Washington on January 5, 1984. Most ED press conferences are sparsely attended, and I was surprised and encouraged by the large press and television turnout. We did not have seats for all those who came.

The reactions were sharp and animated. Reporters obviously focused on their own states, but the national picture interested them too. Those who had been clever enough to pick up an embargoed early copy to study before the conference were the best armed with questions. Some had already contacted their state education departments.

As I expected, we had compliments and brickbats tossed our way. Many complained because we did not have more complete data. Some said releasing the rankings was unfair. But these remarks were countered by others in the audience who described the data as the most complete they had ever seen.

Over the next few days we had hundreds of phone calls from across the nation. Newspapers ran stories on our wall chart that focused on information with implications for state legislation and local school board action. The interest, the curiosity, the debate, the seeking of explanations and answers enriched our nationwide campaign to rally the American people around their schools, to change educational priorities, and to make education public issue number one.

The following year, in early January of 1985, my second wall chart ranking the states on student performance, expenditures, and population characteristics was released to the public. My successor, Secretary William Bennett, continued the practice of publishing an annual ranking of the states releasing his data in February 1986 and February 1987. In each of these four years most of the data were gathered, analyzed, and published using the original format and statistical procedure. But in response to an appeal from state and local education agencies, the method of calculating high school graduation rates in the February 1986 release was changed to adjust for interstate migration of students and students not classified by grade level. Though the other data have been consistently reported for each of the four years, the high school completion data displayed in the charts were calculated on a different basis in 1985 and 1986. Educators and interested parents need to be aware of these changes as they interpret the wall charts from year to year.

Because all states at that time could not provide data on their graduating classes of 1983, we prepared the first wall chart using 1982 statistics. We compared it with state-by-state data for 1972 to show the changes—especially the declines in college entrance exam scores and high school graduation rates—over the past ten years.

Because of the differing minority and inner-city population characteristics, the task of education in some states is much more difficult than in others. To display the diversity among the states with respect to the poverty and minority factors, the states were ranked by per capita income, percentage of school-age population living in poverty, percentage of minority school-age population, and percentage of enrollment classified as handicapped under the guidelines of federal law.

We posted the percentage of high school graduates that took the test so that observers would be aware that a higher proportion of the graduating classes were tested in some states than in others. Though some education test and measurement experts have expressed differing views, the specialists advising me concluded that after class participation reaches twenty percent the statewide average score is no longer affected by increased participation. This point continued to be an item for debate among testing experts until the percentage participation cutoff point was raised to 35 in the February 1984 wall chart.

The gratifying thing about the entire school reform effort started in April of 1983 has been the number of governors who responded aggressively to remedying their states' deficiencies. Governors have been the most effective leaders in reform, and without their political clout the movement would have fizzled out in a few months. Because of their continuing support and the vigilance of the press, chief state school officers, school boards, teachers and parents, the push for renewal of our schools continues.

Where are we today? How much of the impetus generated by *A Nation at Risk* and the widely disseminated state rankings has been sustained? How much has really changed? The results have been mixed with many disappointments as well as encouraging outcomes.

Although some states have made significant progress, nationwide increases in both test scores and graduation rates have not been spectacular since the school reform movement began in 1983. Nationally, ACT scores have risen 2.2 percent and SAT scores 1.5 percent from 1982 to 1986. The high school graduation rate improved slightly during the years 1982 to 1985 (no 1986 data were published in the 1987 release) going from 69.7 percent to 70.6 percent. It does appear that the nineteen-year decline in college entrance scores has been reversed, but I had been confident that we would see more dramatic increases in both college entrance exam scores and high school completion rates. The nation's failure to recover its losses in education performance has been disappointing to me. But the downward slide in education occurred over a period spanning two decades, and it will require a persistent effort over time to recover.

According to an April 1986 tabulation of state education reform efforts compiled by the Education Commission of the States, forty-one states had then raised their high school graduation requirements, thirty-three states had initiated student competency testing, and thirty required teacher competency tests. Also, twenty-four states had initiated career ladder salary programs designed to add the dimension of teacher performance to years of experience and academic credits in determining teachers' salaries. Significantly, all the career ladder programs were mandated and funded by legislative action. Not one state at that time had initiated performance-based pay through the action of a state board of education.

In most of the states in which governors have taken an active role in education, new legislation has been enacted to improve learning, decrease dropout rates, and raise standards and expectations for students. In several of these states, increases in college entrance test scores have been much higher than the gains of the nation as a whole.

The state of South Carolina, for example, attained the greatest gain among the SAT states with an increase from 1982 to 1986 of 36 points, compared to a 13 point national gain over this same period. When it is considered that South Carolina has a 41 percent minority enrollment and 21 percent of its students living in poverty, these data are encouraging. South Carolina, under the leadership of Governor Richard Riley, was one of the first states to pass a comprehensive school reform law and to increase funding for schools. Alabama, with a 36 percent minority enrollment and with 23 percent of its students living in poverty, was the leader among the ACT states in college entrance exam score gains. And the District of Columbia, with a 96 percent minority enrollment and 26 percent of its students living in poverty, was second only to South Carolina in SAT score gains (increasing thirty-one points) from 1982 to 1986.

Though their standings among the states are much higher than Alabama and South Carolina, in California and New York, our two most populous states, the gains in SAT scores have not been as encouraging. Both had shown steep declines in SAT scores, and I had hoped to see a quicker recovery. In 1972, California's SAT score was 957, and New York's was 955. For over ten years these scores fell dramatically in both states, with California hitting a bottom score of 899 and New York 896 in 1982. By 1986 the California score had risen only five points (compared to thirteen for the nation as a whole) to 964, while New York's score over the same time rose only two points to 898. Forty-eight percent of California's school population is minority and 14 percent of the school-age children were living in homes with family incomes below the poverty level. New York's student population was 36 percent minority, and 18 percent of the school-age children were living in poverty.

On the other hand, our lowest achieving state surprised me. Mississippi high school ACT scores in 1986 had increased twice that of the national average score change despite the fact that Mississippi had the highest percentage (30) of its school-age population living in poverty, and 51 percent of the student body were minority children.

Despite the good news and bad emerging from the school reform movement to date, there is reason for optimism because it does seem that necessity is forcing the American people to recognize that the quality of their educational system has a direct bearing on the nation's economic, political, and social well being and its influence abroad. Faced with trade deficits, shoddy goods, unemployed (and unemployable) youth, and other massive problems, we realize that we can no longer ignore the link. Necessity is proving to be a more powerful impetus to reform than persuasion and even eloquence.

But we have a long way to go. In 1985, Minnesota, Nebraska, Iowa, and North Dakota had high school completion rates of over 86 percent. Not more than 14 percent of the high school freshmen dropped out of school prior to graduation. But in the same year, the high school completion rate in Florida, Georgia, Louisiana, and North Carolina never exceeded 63 percent. The probabilities of dropping out of school before high school completion are two-and-a-half times greater in Mississippi than in Iowa. Add that to the college entrance exam score differences and you have an intolerable gap in education performance.

The high school completion–dropout rates in America tell a tragic story of failed child care, child motivation, parental responsibility, and school performance effectiveness. Twenty-nine percent of the youth of America—more than one out of every four students—leave high school before graduation. In this era of limited opportunity for the under-educated and functionally illiterate, the loss of over a quarter of our total population of teenagers is one of the greatest catastrophes imaginable.

In states where there are vast numbers of children living in poverty and where huge minority populations are prevalent, we also have so many single parent or no-parent families in which children are raised in conditions that make learning almost impossible, that the schools there must be given the support necessary to make success more probable. The nation cannot long endure the failure rate experienced in these schools.

Since the release of the rankings of the states, a new trend of openness and candid comparisons has emerged. Several states (Colorado and Oklahoma, for example) are now moving to statewide achievement testing. Also, the Council of Chief State School Officers has launched an effort to compile more acceptable measures of student progress than those represented by college entrance exam scores. And, most notable of all, the Educational Testing Service of Princeton, New Jersey, has a contract with the U.S. Department of Education to conduct the National Assessment of Educational Progress (NAEP) that had been so ably initiated by the Education Commission of the States. These developments promise to give us more accurate information about the states.

I am convinced that one of the keys to increased productivity in our schools is to simply report student achievement regularly, systematically, and with full candor. In most human endeavors, when performance is measured performance improves. We should report on a school-by-school basis, on a school district-by-school district basis, and on a state-by-state basis. We should release openly and frankly all available measures on education. By doing this we share with all those concerned about education the results of our efforts. The yield on the public investment in education will most certainly increase if we become completely candid in reporting student test scores, dropout rates, and other measures.

I have discussed this issue many times with respected colleagues who disagree with me. They continue to complain that tests do not accurately measure all educational outcomes. I agree that tests have their limitations. Low-income and minority students have traditionally scored lower on standardized achievement tests. With this in mind, we should display information about numbers of low income and minority students when publishing test results on our schools. The limitations of our testing should be scrutinized and explained, and we should caution about unwarranted conclusions and unfair criticism. Parents and taxpayers will grasp the implications and the distinctions if we make the effort to explain.

Educators have been too defensive about the schools' performance. We need to share more openly if we are to attain the support we so urgently need. The lowest scoring schools will have the most to gain from this policy. Let's measure achievement as best we can while we explain that our measures have imperfections. Let's release our data in comparative format so schools, neighborhoods, communities and parents all know where they stand.

I have often wondered why we have been so successful in motivating students and attracting public support for athletic accomplishment yet have lacked similar manifestations of enthusiasm from students and parents for academic pursuits. If we took down all the scoreboards at athletic contests and if we shut down the publicity that hails distinguished student performance in sports, the interest would fade. By the same token, if we apply some of the motivation techniques surrounding athletics to our needs in academic pursuits, I am convinced we will attain higher levels of excellence in our schools.

Motivation has always been the major criterion of student learning. We learn how to stimulate students to perform at the outer limits of their ability.

Candor in reporting student achievement is important, but it is only one element in a comprehensive program to help *all* our youth become all they can be. Through *A Nation at Risk* and the publication of state-by-state comparative data we have identified the gaps between what is and what should be in education. How are we to educate *all* our students, both the advantaged and the disadvantaged? The final chapter suggests ways to achieve this.

CHAPTER 11

Ronald Reagan and the School Reform Movement

||||||||||||||||||||||||||||||||||||||||||||||||||||||||||||||||||||||||||||||||||||||||||||||||||||||||||||||||||||||||||||||||||||||||||||

I didn't need polls to tell me that the NCEE report had touched a national nerve, and neither did the president and his staff. I knew how widespread interest in and worry about education had become from the swelling demands on my speaking time. The White House knew it from its mail and the persisting and prominent media coverage of the subject. But since it was preelection season once again and both national and statewide pollsters were out there assessing which issues most concerned the public, we also had concrete documentation of what we already knew.

The president had promised to help disseminate the report and he honored his word; but there was no question that this commitment also accorded with the national mood and further enhanced his great popularity with the voters. Ronald Reagan's presence obviously attracted larger audiences—and higher level participation—than the dissemination conferences would otherwise have drawn, and guaranteed nationwide coverage by the huge White House press corps. One of our early conferences was scheduled for Hopkins, Minnesota, a suburb of Minneapolis, and planning it with the invaluable assistance of Undersecretary Gary L. Jones, I called Governor Rudy Perpich's office to seek his participation. I was told the governor's calendar was full, but happily (and not surprisingly) it cleared a few days later when the president let us know he would like to be on the program.

Most of the commission members were also present, and the shirt-sleeved president joined them in a lively panel discussion that pleased and informed the attentive audience of educators, state legislators, teachers, and students from the multistate region around Minnesota. By separating into small groups after the principal addresses, commission members and listeners had the opportunity of questioning one another vigorously and discussing the data, recommendations, and issues that concerned them all. It was a productive and exhilarating conference in every respect.

There were eleven similar sessions at strategically selected locations around the country, and they were equally successful. They served Ronald Reagan's purposes as well, for it was clear that his participation in an issue of such wide popular concern enhanced his cause in the forthcoming presidential campaign.

The conferences drew wide attention, and my standing in the administration changed dramatically as the acclamations poured in. The *San Diego Union* ran a story under the headline: "My, How the Humble Has Risen." This account described my increased popularity with the top-level hierarchy at the White House, and my so-called frequent flights with the president on *Air Force I*. It also highlighted the appearances I had been making on network TV and the attention paid to my speeches. Then, it poked a little fun at the president for embracing education after his earlier vows to abolish ED.

Publicity like this undoubtedly sent angry tremors through some corridors in the West Wing of the White House but I doubt that they bothered the president a whit. I was obviously delighted to have him on my side, and somewhat startled, as well, to find myself a prominent partner in the dissemination conferences in which he appeared. I was not only asked to be on the platform with him in support of education reform but was invited to fly to some of these occasions on Air Force One. This is a heady experience for any citizen, and for Number Thirteen, so often and for so long reminded painfully of the low esteem in which his agenda was held, it was sweet indeed.

My first trip took us to Kentucky, Kansas City, and Los Angeles. A manifest issued by the Air Force had assigned us seats, given us instructions, and told us about food and other amenities before we boarded the presidential Boeing 707 at Andrews Air Force Base in Maryland.

My assigned seat provided about the same space one has in first-class seating on a commercial airline. The interior of the plane was pleasantly decorated but not elaborate. Indeed, I had expected it to be more lush than it was.

The stewards on board were attentive and provided refreshment of all kinds. The food exceeded the quality and variety offered by the regular airlines. I was billed for all food and beverages after each flight. Being a guest of the president on *Air Force I* did not provide free food and beverages, and this was as it should be.

The president's senior staff has a compartment next to his. Mike Deaver and Jim Baker usually accompanied the president on his trips and so did Ed Meese, but Meese was not on board for any of the trips taken by Ronald Reagan to help in the dissemination of the NCEE report. I never knew if his absence was of his own choosing or at the president's direction.

Deaver was cordial and obviously supportive of my involvement with the president in the school reform efforts. Indeed, I had been told that he was responsible for Ronald Reagan's participation, and that he began pushing for it after reports from polls indicated education to be one of the greatest public concerns.

I was naturally curious about the president's private compartment, but I was never inside it until I flew home from the culminating national dissemination conference in Indianapolis. It was comfortably furnished with a lounge chair, a work station, a sofa, tables, and telecommunications facilities that are in effect a flying switchboard. Sleeping facilities are also on board for long flights. The presidential quarters are pleasant but not in the least lavish.

A government-owned presidential press plane flies on about the same schedule as *Air Force I*. This provides opportunity for newspapers and reporters from the electronic media to supply the public with information about the president and events in which he is involved outside Washington, D.C. A limited number (usually three or four) of reporters are allowed space on *Air Force I*, usually chosen by a method worked out between the press corps and the president's staff. News media people, of course, pay their own expenses connected with presidential travel.

The costs of transporting the president are enormous, largely because of security problems. His bulletproof limousine must be sent ahead by Air Force transport plane, and helicopters must also be transported on many trips. This, plus Secret Service escort vehicles and other equipment, make each presidential junket both complex and costly.

In all the president's discussions of education issues at these conferences, he was responsive to the surprisingly popular content of *A Nation at Risk* and after his speech would take questions from the audience. The most frequent question was about the sharp reduction in education spending that he had included in every budget he sent to Congress.

He handled this issue with his usual adeptness. He emphasized that the funding should come from the states. He claimed that the deep reduction in the federal income tax rates made it possible for states that wanted to put more money into education. The inflation rate that had been eating into all our wallets was subsiding, and the president did not fail to explain how his success in this area helped education budgets.

Notwithstanding his support of the NCEE report, the president hit on one theme with which I strongly disagreed.

"The education problems are not money problems," he would say. "If money alone could solve the problems they would have gone away a long time ago."

He would then go on to explain that federal financial assistance for education had been increased fivefold over two decades. But even at its highest level, federal funding of education never exceeded 8 percent of nationwide education expenditures. The Department of Education budget was approximately $18 billion. This is a large sum, but it is a relatively small part of the total of $240 billion expended on education in 1984.

Moreover, federal funding, despite its relatively small percentage of the total national expenditure, was crucial to those most in need of equal educational opportunity: the handicapped, children from low-income families, and minorities. The impression that we had increased funding for education fivefold was not accurate.

And money *did* matter. Teachers' salaries were a national disgrace. They could not support a decent standard of living in most states. Extensive moonlighting was the result, and this sapped the vitality of teachers carrying heavy loads at school. Salaries affected morale. The best college talent shunned teaching. It takes money to solve this problem; and the low status of the teaching profession was the number one problem in education. The president knew this. I could not hear him say education problems were not money problems without cringing inside as I sat on the platforms listening to him speak.

Despite these disagreements, he helped in many ways. He hit the teacher merit pay issue often, and I was delighted. I also agreed with his call for higher standards, more motivation, and the other issues that had been outlined so eloquently in *A Nation at Risk*.

Our trip to the Kansas City area was the first time I heard these themes expressed, and they were the content of the president's speaking agenda on education as we traveled to various cities across the nation.

After the president's address, I was surprised and pleased to see him participate in a question-and-answer session with the students for an extended period of time. So far as I could determine, the questions were spontaneous. He handled them well, except for one question from a student leader that caused a bit of awkwardness. I had heard it often, but I had never been present when the president himself had to explain his rationale for wanting to abolish the U.S. Department of Education. I listened intently.

There was a somewhat awkward pause while he gathered his thoughts on how to answer. I knew that he wanted to come across as a valiant advocate of schools since this entire three-stop tour to Kentucky, Kansas City, and Los Angeles was centered on our school reform efforts.

He said that he was keenly interested in education and hesitated again. Then he went on to explain that he favored local and state control of schools but feared the ultimate usurpation of schools' governance at the federal level in Washington. This answer was obviously not adequate, for we can have a cabinet-level department without exercising federal control of schools, just as we can have cabinet-level departments of labor, commerce, and health and human services without controlling labor, business, or medicine.

The president's entire discussion of the issue of abolishing the Department of Education was ineffective, evasive, and awkward. He was caught in a conflict between the underlying convictions in his 1980 campaign promise, in which he still believed, and his desire to show leadership responsive to the nationwide bipartisan citizen consensus for improving the effectiveness of education. Since the commission's report was a product of his administration, and since it originated in the very department he had promised to abolish, he was caught in the dilemma of having to be seen to support what he opposed ideologically.

The most effective part of his response was the affirmation of his commitment to retain the traditional federal role of funding college student aid, aid for the handicapped, and financial assistance to schools with concentrations of disadvantaged children from low-income families. He did not mention civil rights enforcement.

In his limousine on our way back to the airport for the flight on to California, the president asked, "Well, did I handle the question on the future of the Department of Education okay?"

I paused for a moment, because I was uncertain about how to answer. I was sitting on the back seat next to him. Mike Deaver was sitting in one of the jump seats facing the president and me.

"I wondered if the question from the student leader surprised you," I said, answering his question with one of my own since I was in a bind too.

"I didn't want to say anything to embarrass you," he replied.

He may not have wanted to embarrass me, but I also knew that he did not want to compromise himself on this issue. To my relief, he did not pursue further the question he posed to me. I did not want to tell him that the question of abolishing the Department of Education was an exercise in futility. He and I both knew that it would never happen. But he had to hold to his campaign promise until after the 1984 election. His radical right friends would be enraged by any denial of this commitment, and the press would home in him and magnify it further.

The president wanted to gain the greatest possible mileage from the commission's report, and I was eager to see him continue to assert the need for school reform. That meant he had to tread a sometimes uncomfortable line between his opposition to a variety of federal roles in education and his endorsement of the very popular report; and it meant that I had to field questions, from both audiences and the press, in ways that would not undercut his views and perhaps make it impossible for him to continue to speak out.

"He's just using you, Ted," my friends complained. "It's all a political game with him. He doesn't care about education, but here he is using your commission and its report for his own political advantage."

I heard this over and over after the issue of school reform emerged. Generally the comments came from critics who didn't like the president. But I respected him despite the obviously different views that naturally emerged from a conservative Republican and a moderate.

"He may be using me," I answered. "But I am doing all I can to use him for my cause and take advantage of his great popularity."

I did, indeed, need the president. We were on a roll in education. We had promises to keep that we had made with the national commission members. Every speech and public appearance on the education problem of the day placed Ronald Reagan out front.

Happily, neither the president nor I had any problems with another means of highlighting school reform. Not long after the commission's report was released, I set out to find the best secondary schools across the nation. We launched the secondary school recognition program to honor these schools. We wanted to feature them to show the public that excellence was attainable under current circumstances. We needed role models. We especially needed schools with large concentrations of low-income and minority students who were defying the odds and swimming successfully against "the rising tide of mediocrity."

We asked the state departments of education to nominate a select few of their best schools. A thirty-two member secondary-school recognition panel reviewed these institutions, visiting them and choosing only those that were truly distinguished. I appointed the membership of this panel from a list of outstanding authorities on secondary education.

I was surprised to learn how eagerly schools sought one of these national awards. They wanted to be recognized as exemplary. We had designed a special flag to be flown on the flagpoles of the designated schools below the American flag. With the great seal of the United States and "Excellence in Education" proclaimed across it, it was a source of great pride to those schools, students, and communities that won the honor.

An interesting by-product of the school recognition effort was the response from realtors and local chambers of commerce. Because of the publicity associated with the awards, many newly arrived residents in a community asked realtors to locate a home for them that was inside the attendance boundary of a nationally recognized school. The Department of Education was unwittingly affecting real estate values.

Pioneer High School in Whittier, California, in Orange County south of Los Angeles, was one of the schools chosen to be honored, and the president agreed to present it with its Excellence in Education flag. We flew to Los Angeles on *Air Force I* after his Kansas City appearance. I got up early the next day for a 5 A.M. appearance on the "Today Show," visited a vocational education center in Orange County later that morning, and was in Whittier for the afternoon presentation ceremony.

Pioneer High School is a remarkable institution. It serves an area populated chiefly by low-income Hispanic families, a situation that presumably could have made it yet another typical depressed area public school infested with drugs, high dropout rates, teenage crime, and violence. Not so. Pioneer is virtually an educational miracle. What I saw there convinced me that our method of identifying the nation's most outstanding schools had been effective.

As a rule there is a high correlation between income levels of families and academic achievement of students. Students from affluent areas are often highly motivated, capable, and committed to attaining high levels of achievement. Conversely, students from low-income areas are often characterized by apathy; and dropout rates in their schools are big, with student achievement seeming to reflect the discouragement of their low-income or unemployed families.

The principal of Pioneer High School, Robert Eicholtz, was a very dynamic, personable educator. He did not accept assumptions such as these, believing that his students were just as capable as those in more affluent areas. He had high expectations and demanding standards for both students and faculty. He knew how to motivate them to reach for their best. His demeanor was upbeat, positive, and confident. He established an atmosphere of creative tension without excessive pressure.

He used every moment of his day to be in touch with faculty, students, and parents. His purpose was motivation, generated by recognition of accomplishment, and persuasion that working hard was the price they had to pay for success. His leadership style and his personality were evident in every cranny of Pioneer High School. But he also went beyond the school, reaching out to the neighborhoods and parents to enlist them in programs and the aims of his school.

He was not only a general, he was a one-man army fighting for the cause of learning. He loved his students and appreciated and respected his teachers. He knew that education extended beyond his school, and he took measures to see that the power and influence of Pioneer High followed his students into their homes.

My observation of this school and the others that were honored in our nationwide recognition program convinces me that the principal is the key to school improvement. I did not see a single school that qualified for our award that was not led by a dynamic and persuasive principal.

More care in selecting principals and more time spent in evaluating and training them will yield great dividends in learning. Too many principals do not lead their schools; they simply tend the store and maintain the status quo. Students, parents, and communities pay a heavy price when they have to endure mediocre schools led by mediocre principals.

The recognition and award ceremony at Pioneer High was a huge success. The high school gymnasium was packed with students, parents, and community leaders. A visit from the president of the United States to honor their school provided thousands of Hispanic parents and children an opportunity to demonstrate their civic pride and commitment to learning. The enormous White House press corps ensured that the honoring of Pioneer High had an impact across the nation.

The dramatic moment when we presented the flag to the principal and student leaders was leavened by some unexpected, slightly embarrassing humor. We had invited David Gardner to come down from Berkeley, where he was now serving in his new position as president of the University of California; and he, I, and President Reagan made brief remarks to the huge audience. Then the president and I proceeded to unfurl the Excellence in Education flag and hold it up before the audience and all the TV cameras. Because of the way the banner had been folded, and because I didn't check it prior to our displaying it, the president and I unfurled a flag that was not only upside down but backwards.

Naturally, the audience laughed at the goof. Even after we corrected the upside-down display, the flag was backwards, and they roared again. But Ronald Reagan, always poised and unflappable, turned the whole episode into an opportunity to help everyone laugh some more. It was an incident that demonstrated why he is so popular and why so many people esteem him even when they disagree with his policies. He's personable and likable. That's why he could cut my budget and still keep my respect. It was a strange phenomenon and one I never did fully understand.

Since Pioneer High School received substantial federal funding for its low-income and handicapped students, I used the Pioneer High School episode to underscore to the president the value of the federal aid programs that he had repeatedly tried to eliminate in his proposals to Congress. I also described the federally subsidized school lunch program that provides nutrition to children being raised in poverty. Students cannot learn when they are hungry, malnourished, and half-sick most of the time. I pointed out the way in which all these efforts to supplement but not supplant what the states and local school districts were doing really helped us to cut back on future federally funded welfare bills. This was a teaching opportunity for me, and I used it to firm up the commitments I heard from the president in Kansas City.

It made so much sense to invest in human capital and the future potential of all the children of the nation that I was sure I could persuade the president to do more for the nation's schools and colleges.

My concern for the low-income and disadvantaged students in elementary and secondary students extends on to college. College is expensive. Low-income students have no hope for education beyond high school without financial assistance in the form of grants, loans, and work-study programs. David Stockman had been slashing at this source of assistance like a wild dog. I knew from my own desperate needs as a youth raised in poverty that millions had to have this help or abandon their dreams. If I failed to do everything I could on behalf of these millions of needy youth, the burden of their disillusionment would fall on me.

Our last big hurrah in disseminating the message of *A Nation at Risk* took place in Indianapolis at a final national conference on excellence in education. Governor Bob Orr helped host this event, which we planned as a climax and summation of the twelve regional sessions we had held across the country.

This conference attracted many governors who had been the most distinguished leaders in educational reform in their states, and most of those with the power and influence to formulate education policy and steer new directions in education. These included college presidents, college deans, school superintendents, leaders of governing boards, heads of national organizations, chief state school officers, leading lawmakers on the national as well as the state level, and business executives.

Representatives from the White House participated with ED's senior staff in organizing the conference because the president had agreed to address the final session. We selected speakers with reputations as authorities in their fields. We put together the stimulating groups of individuals as panel participants.

On the last night of the conference, President Reagan, his staff, and the White House press entourage flew into town. I approached the evening with my inevitable concern about what he would say in the major address that his speech writers had prepared for him. I had been burned often enough by the ideologues not to be sanguine, despite the positive content of the advance text. Since this was to be a major address and his last in the dissemination series, I wondered if they would write a substitute speech as they had done back in April when the NCEE report was released at the White House.

The plan for the evening was that I would address the audience as the first speaker. Then, we would have a short recess to set up the TV cameras and prepare for the president's appearance.

Following my speech, Governor Orr appeared on stage with the president, and before the television cameras he introduced me. Much to my surprise, the audience gave me a standing ovation. Then it was my turn to introduce the president.

He had been out on the circuit with me. He had given great support each time I needed it the most. Except for the script from his hard-right speech writers when the report was released, the president had been a fantastic endorser of our efforts to build momentum for school reform. And much to my relief he did it again. He kept to his prepared text. It emphasized the stakes involved in the outcome of our school reform efforts. He had several effective phrases that would make news and should touch Americans as they thought about the education of their children.

When he finished the audience gave him a standing ovation. I breathed a sigh of relief. The event had gone over well. It marked the successful culmination of our long campaign to disseminate *A Nation at Risk.* I was very pleased, and my weariness was the happy kind that comes when a job has been well done.

Jim Baker invited me to fly back to Washington with the president on *Air Force I,* and I was surprised and pleased to be invited to ride in the compartment of the plane reserved for the president's senior executives. My conversation with Jim Baker and Mike Deaver gave me an opportunity to assess our progress. Jim had been a source of significant support to me since I first met him back in January of 1981. Deaver's duties called for little contact with cabinet members, but his participation in and support of the president's junkets to help push school reform gave me a chance to learn that he was not ideologically in league with the rabid right nor hostile to ED.

From the beginning of our series of dissemination conferences, there were overtones of the 1984 election, as I have noted, and after Indianapolis I was immediately involved in the election campaign. It was a new experience, for I had never run for office. Indeed, I had tried to be nonpartisan in all my state and local administrative roles.

In the early stages of the 1984 campaign two good friends from my home state of Utah came to Washington to try to persuade me to run for governor. I had the name identification. I had years of experience in public life. The idea seemed attractive to me until I began realistically to appraise the ordeal of being a candidate and the time and pressures involved. I had seen enough of the 1982 campaign, and 1984, a presidential year, would be even more extended. I could not bring myself to become a candidate.

Few people realize the sacrifices made by those who choose to run for office. A good many run for selfish reasons, but most sincerely desire to serve their country and the people their office represents. So many politicians become bruised, battered, and burned out that it is a wonder that we attract as many able leaders as we do.

The Republican National Convention was held in Dallas in August. Because I was a member of the president's cabinet, Betty and I were provided with special seating at the general sessions of the convention and invitations to many events, receptions, and dinners.

Though I had watched earlier conventions on TV, they could not prepare me for the reality of the hoopla, the fanfare, the noise, the posturing before network cameras. It was shoddy and third-rate, the tacky kind of showmanship seen at circuses. Perhaps it was fun for others. Maybe those who led the big extravaganza enjoyed it, for it gave them a chance to let themselves go. But the fancy hats, noisemakers, and other devices used in demonstrations seemed less than dignified. After all, we were there to select candidates whom we would propose to the American people as their leaders for four years.

I realize that the fun and noisiness do not necessarily mean that serious people do not get down to hard and productive work after having had a riotously good time at a convention that convenes only once every four years. Perhaps these sentiments are simply the emotional accoutrements of a man with white hair obsessed with too many concerns about dignity and civility. I only know that for me there seemed to be an atmosphere of phoniness and hucksterism surrounding the convention.

The big prize was of course a foregone conclusion. No one even hinted that we would not nominate Ronald Reagan and George Bush, so the convention was devoid of much tension about the outcome.

Reservations had been made at the Anatole Hotel for the cabinet members and their wives. The rooms were paid for by the Republican National Committee, and each secretary paid all other costs such as food, travel, and entertainment. We had a bird's-eye view of all events, and the cabinet box was a busy place. I worked with a group of cabinet colleagues who appeared before a number of state caucuses on behalf of the president and his candidacy for renomination. My task was to give a short talk about education and then field questions.

During the convention preliminaries the platform committee struggled with the issue of the future of the U.S. Department of Education. I knew it was crucial that my party not renew its 1980 platform pledge to abolish the department. It would be a futile and destructive exercise, and of all the actions to be taken at the convention, I earnestly hoped that the Republicans would not take up that fight again.

A Nation at Risk placed educational reform high on the public opinion agenda, and this had its political payoff for the president. He stole the issue from Walter Mondale, and it cost us nothing in the budget. It was simply a splendid issue to use in the domestic affairs arena, for it obscured concern about cuts in welfare, aid to dependent children, Medicaid, and other social program reductions. It had such broad-based national and popular support that by the time the Republican Platform Committee addressed the issue, it was clear that any move that even hinted it might be antieducation was doomed.

Given this, the far right did not have a chance. The platform committee wanted no part of a move to put abolition of the Education Department back in the 1984 platform. Republican delegates who were serving in the U.S. House of Representatives deserve most of the credit for rejecting any push to put the abolition of ED back on the list of campaign planks. Many of them were solid, responsible conservatives who had the wisdom to know that the party would be hurt. We won by an impressive vote of six to one when the matter came up. It was a victory to savor, and I enjoyed it thoroughly.

Inevitably, a member of Ed Meese's staff told me that the platform victory and the president's silence about it should not give me any cause to celebrate. He quoted Meese assuring his people that the fight to abolish ED would be renewed after the election despite the decisive rejection by the convention in Dallas. I considered this simply as mumblings from those who had suffered a humiliating defeat. I knew the U.S.

Department of Education was now a permanent cabinet-level agency in the federal structure. I celebrated this crucial turning point that assured that neither major political party would be mounting a further serious effort to demote its status in the federal governmental structure.

As a cabinet member I was expected to campaign for Ronald Reagan's reelection. What is more, the Republican National Committee also wanted the support of the cabinet in congressional, senatorial, and gubernatorial races. I had to sharpen my political campaign skills, and since they were virtually nonexistent, this required some serious honing on my part.

Even before the Democratic convention it was virtually certain that former Vice President Walter Mondale would be the standard-bearer for the Democrats. He had been a stalwart supporter of education during his years as a U.S. senator from Minnesota, and during my days in HEW as the U.S. commissioner of education I had several occasions to call on Fritz Mondale for aid. He was always gracious, intelligent in his responses, and eager to help schools and colleges. My only problem with him was his liberal stance and his failure to understand the necessity to limit the federal role in education to providing leadership and supplemental financial assistance, while leaving the management and control of schools and colleges to state and local authorities.

The Republican National Committee assembled a book entitled *Vice President Malaise: Twenty Years of Walter Mondale*. (The opposition put together literature in a similar vein on Ronald Reagan.) This book was given to me as a resource to be used during the campaign. The front cover featured a scowling, sneering Mondale countenance. It was absolutely the ugliest picture of Fritz that I had ever seen. Inside the cover of the book was the photo credit: "Cover photograph courtesy of AP World Wide Photos." It reminded me of some ghastly shots of me, taken at my worst, that had appeared in the press at times when I was being depicted in a bad light.

The first page of the text was a quote from Mondale in the *Minneapolis Star* that had run back on June 15, 1970: "Our priorities are pretty close to being obscene." The comment under this quotation read: "Walter Mondale has never offered Americans a vision of the future that is optimistic or inspires confidence. He has built his public career by trashing America."

The contents included quotes, data on his voting record, and details of his various actions as vice president and U.S. senator. It had all the ammunition a political gunfighter would need to rip into his opponent.

I blanched at the meanness of the prose, my introduction to the seamy side of political campaigning. It did not take me long, however, to find opposition literature that was just as nasty and mean spirited. All civility goes out the window when Republicans and Democrats square off to contend for office.

The British are a bit more polite, but I have observed that political candidates there and in most other democracies as well can get nasty too and sling equally nasty mud. But our campaigns stand out in two respects: They demonstrate much more rudeness and bad manners. They are also interminable, and their garrulousness make them seem even longer.

Never was this more apparent to me than in the 1984 election season. I was called upon to campaign for senators, members of congress, and governors. I was out in the hills, cities, and villages of West Virginia. I campaigned in Idaho and Oregon. In all of this I found my behavior spurious and my words tainted with a touch of phoniness regardless of my efforts to present an intellectually honest discussion of the issues. I realized that I had to support a Republican candidate, warts and all. This included speaking after a candidate's remarks had extolled the virtues of actions previously taken that were anathema to me, such as slashing funds for the poor, for student aid, and for health care for the aged.

In a few of the races I found good friends contending with each other. When these contests degenerated into the verbal squalor that often develops when a race is close, I felt the deepest revulsion. In no case did I note this with more sorrow than in the Illinois senatorial race between incumbent Charles Percy and Democratic Congressman Paul Simon. It befitted neither of them.

Immediately after the president was reelected by a very impressive majority on November 1, the distasteful process of campaigning was behind me and a new urgency replaced it. It was budget time. With the election behind us, all the principals in the administration had to move ahead on a very fast track to ready our proposals for the 1985–86 fiscal year that began on October 1, 1985. Once again I was in confrontation with OMB Director David Stockman.

The players were no different than in previous years, but the game of deliberate leaking was much more intense than usual. The leaks came, I knew, from high-placed sources to upper-level people in the conservative press. My confidential budget proposals were publicized unfavorably in several publications. The sources had to be either OMB itself or the White House—meaning Ed Meese's people.

When I challenged Stockman on this violation of confidence, I learned that Meese himself had requested early copies of what I had submitted.

It was time for a confrontation on this matter, and I used the president's budget review committee to get the matter before its members, Jim Baker, Ed Meese, and David Stockman.

We met in the Roosevelt Room in the West Wing for my presentation of the Department of Education appeal. I had been in a slow burn for several days. Along with Meese, Baker, and Stockman, the room was filled with the usual number of onlookers.

Instead of talking about budget numbers, I opened with a strong protest at the leaks. They were intended to do as much harm as possible, and I was not going to take it. I was furious by now, and I came on strong, shouting and pounding the table. My anger was directed at Meese and Stockman and their denial in the face of the obvious.

After I finished with ethics and keeping confidences, I turned to the budget. My appeals to restore the OMB cuts got nowhere. The dollar amounts were not going to be raised. The federal deficit would have justified the slashing if the priorities had been fair and evenhanded with respect to other departments, but this was not the case. ED had been singled out. Even my proposal to rearrange the dollar allocations while keeping within my budget allowance was rebuffed.

I left the Roosevelt Room angrier than ever, and knew that I had incurred the wrath and open enmity of both Meese and Stockman. But most important, the budget review episode made it clear that the President's second term would not continue the high-priority attention that education had enjoyed since April of 1983. David Stockman made that plain in a budget discussion with me that was in sharp contrast to his remarks a few months earlier. I had not forgotten his telling the cabinet that the "sensitive area of education" would be the one department to whom the budget "targets" would not apply. There, he had said, we would want to "stay out front."

What had changed so suddenly? How could the so-called sensitive area of education become such a low priority in such a short time? The only difference was that the election was over. We had won our mandate from the people for a second term. *A Nation at Risk* had served its purpose: Our campaign for a nationwide school reform movement to implement the report's recommendations helped in the campaign for reelection.

Those long time friends with whom I had worked prior to my appointment to the Reagan cabinet had been telling me since April 1983 that the president's commitment to the school reform effort was inspired by political opportunism and that it would come to an abrupt halt after the 1984 election. I refused to believe them. I had heard the president speak persuasively and with too much conviction to think that I would see the last of his efforts once he had won his second term. But with a sour taste in my mouth I had to acknowledge that my friends had been right after all. The commitment lasted only as long as the election season: There was no longer a need to "stay out front" on the "sensitive area of education."

The recognition from the president and the party was great while it lasted. Indeed, the Republican National Chairman, Frank Fahrenkopf, Jr., had introduced me once in Dallas early in 1984 as "the second most important man in this administration." Ironically, the president sent over to my office a beautifully framed copy of the *A Nation at Risk* report. Under it, written in his own handwriting was praise for my work that I did not fully deserve. It read: "In deep appreciation of your leadership which has changed the course of history in American education. Ronald Reagan."

We would have changed the course of history in American education had the president stayed with us through the implementation phase of the school reform movement. And this would have won a place in history for Ronald Reagan as the man who renewed and reformed education at a time when the nation was, indeed, at risk because we were not adequately educating our people to live effectively and competitively in the twenty-first century.

I remembered words of Voltaire I had read long ago: "Every success sharpens the sting of later defeats." In politics and in Washington, I decided, this was all too true.

CHAPTER 12

Parting Words of Number Thirteen

Over the four years of the president's first term, I had seesawed often about staying in the cabinet or finding the right time to leave on my own initiative, depending on how hopeful I was able to be or how discouraged I became. But there was enough that was positive after the release of the commission's report and the president's endorsement of education reform throughout his campaign for me to think I *could* make a difference in the next four years. It was important to keep the extreme right faction from taking charge of ED—especially after my angry confrontation with Meese and Stockman—and it was important to sustain the momentum for reform that had begun so promisingly.

My most pressing concern was a long-standing personal business problem back home in Utah and I had told Jim Baker I might have to leave the cabinet to settle it. But it resolved itself unexpectedly soon after the election, so I went back to Baker's office to tell him I was now planning to stay. I wanted at least two years. They could make a big difference in progress for reform.

There was a decided absence of eagerness at this news. It wasn't that anyone demanded that I resign. But the message seemed clear: a warning to me that the old agenda for ED still prevailed. Regardless of the convention platform decision, the president intended to push for its abolition. From what Jim said, he was also going to insist on those deep budget slashes.

There was simply no commitment to a federal leadership role to assist the states and their local school districts in carrying out the recommendations of *A Nation at Risk*.

Ronald Reagan was unable to recognize that ED could perform that role and exercise crucial oversight while leaving responsibility for the governance of education to the states and local communities. He saw it as either-or: federal control or state and local control. Those fifty-one major speeches in which he had impressed the American people with the vital importance of education and the need for reform had been such a splendid beginning—and that was all there was going to be.

I rode back across town from the White House with Jim Baker's words ringing in my ears. My obligation to support the president's policies would make my position in his cabinet appallingly difficult. How could I turn from all we had planned to further budget cuts and a new bill to abolish ED? Yet Baker had made it clear this would be my charge during the new term.

We had made a brave new beginning. We had won the election. But all that was past now. I would be of little use to the president given his second-term agenda for education; indeed, I would be a problem.

I left my office early and went home to a sleepless night. Early the next morning I sat down at my desk, wrote out my resignation, and sent it over to the president by special courier.

I never heard a word. No one telephoned. Three days later the president announced to the press that I had resigned for personal reasons.

With a sick heart I went through the agony of the farewell parties, the banquet held in my honor. But the most difficult of all was the departure ceremony in the Roosevelt Room in the West Wing of the White House, where the president gave me a going-away present and said:

> Ted Bell has come into a position here and exerted a leadership role at the federal level which, at the time, did not in any way impose or interfere with local and state jurisdictions.
>
> He took the reports of the Commission on Excellence in Education and carried them nationwide to the place that changes have been made at state and local levels that will have a bearing on children for years to come.
>
> Very seldom has a person been able to come into a position for about four years and in those four years see tangible evidence of success as he is able to see as he leaves us now.
>
> He has been Secretary of Excellence.

I could take no joy in this. What the president was hailing me for would soon be negated or abandoned. My term in the cabinet was over.

We made plans to move back to Salt Lake City where I would be a professor at the University of Utah. I would rejoin the academic world in January 1985, as the winter quarter opened. It was U-Haul time again. Betty and I had a lot to do in a short time. A drive across the country in the cold of winter is always a sobering experience. My mood matched the cold, gray weather as we planned another departure from the capital. I was going home from Washington for the third time.

Conflicting emotions chased around in my head. I certainly felt relief—indeed, pleasure—at the prospect of being back in a university community, and in a world characterized at least some of the time by common sense, proportion, and recognition that life for most people is lived in settings more like Salt Lake City (or Chicago or Pocatello or even Lava Hot Springs) than Washington, D.C. But I had a nagging feeling of betrayal that I tried hard to shake off: Promises I thought had been made that had not been kept. I felt frustration at not having been able to secure an enduring commitment to the cause of education at the highest federal level. But most of all I was apprehensive about the future of this cause. Despite rhetoric to the contrary, I knew the enormous popular response to the commission report meant that ED's cabinet status was not reversible. But if my tenure as secretary had taught me anything, it was that a hostile faction in a position of power in the West Wing *could* weaken or even negate both the authority and the programs of the Department of Education.

How could we be confident that supporters of education reform— in the Congress, in other branches of government, in statehouses and legislatures, in the education community, in cities and towns, on local school boards, and among parents and other thoughtful citizens—would be able to sustain the fight against such skillful opposition? Without strong leadership at the federal level I thought their chances shaky; and the nature of my leaving made it obvious that the next secretary of education would have a very different agenda from mine.

So I left for Utah filled with unease. But never about the importance of what I had been fighting for and have continued to fight for. The time since Washington has given me perspective, some cause for optimism—the momentum that followed the commission's report has swelled, not abated—and further ideas about what we need to do to move ahead toward our goal of excellence.

A major goal for every American should be to become more fully independent. Dependence is a deplorable condition. Self-reliance and independence are the foundations of liberty.

The purpose of education is to make this independence and self-sufficiency possible. This should also be the goal of government and the objective of its programs. Federal assistance should build the capacity and strength to be free and productive. Education is a better investment than most of the other areas in which government spends its money because it enhances intelligence and diminishes dependence. Government can do nothing more important than to support education in a manner that encourages these outcomes.

Well-meaning conservatives who have attacked education funding, as well as other programs of federal financial assistance, fail to see the difference between the investment in education that pays the richest of all dividends to our country and other objects of federal expenditure that drain the taxpayers and pay back little or no return. They fail to understand that education is the only way to make big government small and dependent people independent.

Education has another benefit as well. In my four years in his cabinet I was not able to persuade President Reagan to see the connection between education and his first priority of building our military power. He called our new and sophisticated weapons "peacekeepers." I wanted him to acknowledge that intelligent people are peacekeepers too. Secretary of Defense Weinberger understood the connection, and he was always eager to speak up in my often futile effort to defend my budget against the onslaughts of Stockman and OMB. His years as secretary of HEW and his Department of Defense experience with semiliterate recruits in the military services convinced him of the need for excellence in education. Unhappily, this support, welcome as it was, had no real impact.

Ronald Reagan's second priority was to build our economy and get the great American industrial engine up to full capacity. He was constantly speaking to us in cabinet meetings about the power of an open, fully competitive marketplace. He wanted to lift restraints, cut back government regulation, and emphasize the supply side of the economic equation. Hard work, increases in productivity, and reward for effort were major elements of the Reagan credo. He knew that freedom and a high standard of living would not be preserved without economic as well as military strength.

But the aspirations and freedom of our people rest not only on our productivity and our military capacity but also on our talent and intelligence. Intelligence, creativity, and increased productivity are tied irrevocably to education. The future will belong to the intelligent. We must work hard, but we must also work smart. I tried to convince the president and his people of the bonds that tie together education, the economy, and military strength. But notwithstanding the fact that I had been a teacher for much of my adult life, I never succeeded in getting this lesson across to them.

In April of 1983, *A Nation at Risk* linked education to the international scene, the economy, and the nation's security. The country's deplorable performance in educating its people for a high-tech information society was eloquently described.

The president did a magnificent job of conveying the necessity of changing this once he took up the crusade, and his help in dissemination of the report was crucial to our success in launching the school reform movement. Without this we would never have attained the momentum we so urgently needed. But when I think today of where we could have been at the conclusion of his second term, I do feel a deep sense of loss. In my mind, nothing could have assured Ronald Reagan's place in history more than his enduring commitment to the school reform movement that he supported so effectively for eighteen months, only to abandon it after the election.

What has happened over the years since the commission's report was released? We should be heartened by some encouraging changes, but we should be deeply concerned about continuing serious deficiencies.

Since the school reform movement began in 1983, we have witnessed significant progress in our schools. The slide in college entrance exam scores has stopped, and some states have made substantial gains. High school graduation requirements have been increased dramatically, and there is somewhat more emphasis on mathematics and science. Teacher education and certification standards are more rigorous, and at least thirty states have taken steps to build career ladders for teachers that reward distinguished teaching performance in the salary structure. State-wide competency testing for both students and entry-level teachers is now practiced in many states. A widespread move to use computers and other electronic technology to teach the basic skills is receiving increasing public funding. The content of our textbooks and supplementary teaching materials is improving. From all these recent changes it is clear that we have made significant strides. We are educating 60 to 70 percent of the youth of America better than in previous decades.

But we have made no progress in reaching, motivating, and teaching the 30 to 40 percent who either drop out before high school graduation or gain their diplomas with at most marginal skills. Many of these persons are from low-income families, and huge numbers reside in urban ghettos. A great many are poor blacks and Hispanics who grow up with little motivation, hope, or real-life acquaintance with success.

Minority youth employment now surpasses the 40 percent level. Teenage pregnancy, which results in the burdens of lost youth and welfare dependence, adds to the tragic circumstances of those who quit school never having been educated to the point of employability. Many of these young people have grown up in welfare-supported families, and we have the phenomenon of third- and even fourth-generation welfare recipients scattered around the nation. Hopelessness breeds hopelessness. If these children are to have a future, this cycle must be broken.

Despite the improvements in our educational system, the figures noted above mean that one-third or more of the nation's youth enter our society without the basic knowledge and skills they need to achieve independence and self-sufficiency—those hallmarks of democratic citizenship. Education means opportunity. For them, and for many others, access to that opportunity has been curtailed or denied. There are fifty million American families in which no member has ever earned a college degree, though obviously there are many among them capable of becoming engineers, teachers, and businesspeople, and of contributing their intelligence and knowledge to our complex society.

Its people are America's richest resource. Its young are America's future. The waste or loss of so many of these young is a blight on that future. Only education can change this. And to do this, education must change.

We are approaching another presidential election and a new era lies ahead. For the next president and for candidates for public office on all levels—federal, state, and local—here is my program for launching change in American education.

Failure to educate millions of our people adequately will move us toward disaster if we do not alter course. There is no higher priority for the new administration. The masses of illiterate and unemployable Americans in our midst represent the number one problem in the United States.

We must launch a nationwide movement of the magnitude of the Marshall Plan that helped rebuild the war-ravaged nations of Europe at the end of World War II. Just as President Truman led us in the revitalization of Europe, and as President Kennedy announced the goal of landing a man on the moon and rallied the American people in support of the endeavor, so should our new president declare that we must reshape education so that the dropout rate is below 5 percent, illiteracy is wiped out, and competence, employability, and adaptability characterize all Americans completing school, regardless of race, ethnic background, or economic status. The administration's goal should be an education system that is the most productive, efficient, and cost-effective in the world.

The new president should make it clear to everyone that the current level of performance in education threatens our very future as a nation. To reach that goal will require all Americans to change their priorities. It will take sacrifice. We launched the Marshall Plan to rebuild the devastated European economy because we knew it was in the best interest of peace and prosperity not only for America but for the free world. The same self-interest and world interest should govern the need to reform and renew education in America.

Under the leadership of the president, and with the support of the Congress, the states and local communities should be galvanized into a nationwide program that restructures and renews teaching and learning in our homes as well as our schools.

To launch a campaign of the magnitude necessary to transform American education, early in his first term the new president should call a summit conference at which he lays out to those present and to the nation the goals that must be attained and how this is to be brought about. Participants should include the country's governors, leading lawmakers from the Congress and the state legislatures, college presidents, school administrators, school board leaders, prominent members of the American Federation of Teachers and the National Education Association, leaders from the national associations of elementary and secondary school principals, and representatives of parent groups.

Basic performance goals should include sharp reduction of the dropout rate, elimination of illiteracy, development of a skilled and competitive work force in which intelligence and creativity are valued, improved mathematical and technological competence, and recruitment of a talented cadre of teachers. To the extent possible, all these goals should be quantified so that yearly progress nationwide can be measured.

The following agenda for action lays out where we need to go and what we need to do to get there.

New Attitudes

Too often "support" for education and recognition of its importance are no more than lip service, obligatory testimonials to a process too familiar to invite real scrutiny. In fact there is a huge discrepancy between what we say we endorse and our real attitudes. We need only look at our past to realize how these attitudes have changed.

The first generation of children of immigrant families in the late nineteenth and early twentieth centuries were unusually successful in their newly adopted country because their parents recognized that education was the path to Americanization, achievement, and a good life. Eastern European Jews whose parents fled czarist tyranny, for example, contributed mightily to the nation's productivity and creativity, and many of our most distinguished scientists, artists, engineers, and entrepreneurs came of this ethnic stock. The astonishing performance of immigrants from the Scandinavian countries helped convert the Midwest into a richly productive agricultural and industrial region. For all these people, and for many others like them, the schools and colleges were *the* springboard to enlightenment, civility, and prosperity. The unswerving obligation of every child was to learn, and as eking out the best living possible was their parents' work, so diligent effort in school was theirs.

Today's young immigrant high achievers are recent arrivals from Asia. Their families, too, look to education as the pathway. The children's mastery of language, mathematics, the sciences, and engineering has been especially notable, and the rapidity with which they have adapted to a new and wholly unfamiliar culture is a further tribute to their motivation.

But if we are frank with ourselves, we must acknowledge that for most Americans—both those whose families have been here longest and those who are the third- and fourth-generation descendants of the hordes who emigrated here before World War I—neither diligence in learning nor rigorous standards of performance prevail. This is the "rising tide of mediocrity" described in *A Nation at Risk,* and the consequences are not only ominous for the future, they are being felt in the present.

How do we once again become a nation of learners, in which attitudes toward intellectual pursuit and quality of work have excellence as their core? Ultimately this will rest with us, the country's citizens; but the genesis for change must come from those we elect to lead us. Widespread though popular dissatisfaction with the quality of American education is, it will remain fragmented, and underlying attitudes will be unlikely to shift unless there is leadership at the top. The rallying cry, the basic program for an educational renaissance, and the provision of resources to implement that program must begin there. It is the president, the fifty governors, and our leading lawmakers who must commit themselves, and us, to action.

With such a commitment, that action becomes the responsibility of all who contribute to and participate in the educational system, whether providing leadership, governance, oversight, funding, curriculum, teaching, performance assessment, or support functions. Though all these are addressed below, it should not be forgotten that parents, students, and concerned citizens are also indispensable participants in this system and initiators of change.

Curriculum

Curriculum is the heart of an education system, and content, standards, and expectations need major revision. Its goal is to provide a sound general education for all Americans, one that prepares them to live freely and perform ably in a rapidly changing, technologically complex, interdependent world. To do this they must be learners, critical thinkers, and competitive workers capable of adapting to new circumstances and new knowledge.

Mastery of the English language is the number one requirement. Students must be able to read with power, speed, and comprehension and write and speak with clarity, order, and precision. Language mastery is the key to communication, judgment, problem solving, and access to the new knowledge that is constantly being generated in today's society.

Therefore English must be studied every year, from kindergarten through the twelfth grade, if *real* literacy is to be achieved. Course content must be rigorous, and it will take school-board-imposed requirements to ensure this. There must be mandatory reading lists that include many of the classics of English and world literature. Optional reading lists should allow choices that enable students to pursue special interests in depth.

Required frequent essay writing is also essential, and while the level of content obviously depends on age and grade level, students should be consistently held to high standards of clarity, grammatical precision, vocabulary, and logic. Writing that is competent in style and effective in content is unrivaled in developing trained intelligence. Even the youngest children take pleasure in expressing themselves in writing and are eager to do their best and respond to helpful guidance. That eagerness should be the start of twelve years of training in written English.

Similar standards of scrupulousness in spoken English are essential too. Oral presentations in the classroom, whether formal or casual, are too often thought of as separate from English as a curriculum subject. While teachers should respect their students' sensibilities in correcting them before others, it does them no service to ignore errors or sloppiness. The ability to express oneself accurately, intelligently, and effectively is crucial to performing well in the workplace, and it is profoundly unfair to young people to neglect this aspect of their education.

It should be noted that written and spoken expression should be held to this high standard in all subjects, not only English. The teacher of history or science must not ignore errors in usage because the course focus is different. Teachers fail in their obligations as teachers if they do this.

School districts should prescribe a minimum number of books a year to be read in order for students to advance to the next grade level and set standards for writing as well. If teacher loads are too heavy to enable them to read and correct essays and discuss the books students have read in order to certify that they have met the school board's requirements for advancement to the next grade, it may be necessary—and desirable—to recruit volunteers from the community (usually parents or other interested and qualified adults) to serve as mentors to the students. This procedure, performed under the direction of the school, is an effective and appropriate way of working with children that permits thoughtful evaluation of their work as well as offers help for overburdened teachers.

Computers are now an integral part of the work involved in writing, for word processing, editing, and checking grammar and spelling. Schools have been slow to use computers in teaching and learning, but to implement the English curriculum above, it will be essential to take advantage of their technology in teaching children on an individual basis and in helping to give them feedback on their progress.

Knowledge of mathematics is indispensable to functioning in the workplace and in daily living, and ignorance of basic skills is shockingly prevalent. Mathematics should be required every year from elementary through the intermediate or junior high school level. At least three years of mathematics should be required for graduation from high school, but the high school curriculum should be adapted to the students' interests, abilities, and plans for work or for college after graduation. College-bound students should take algebra, geometry, trigonometry, and calculus. Students who will work directly after graduation need more basic mastery, including training in the fundamentals of algebra, that will serve them in applied learning situations.

In no other part of the school curriculum is it so natural to use computers as in mathematics. Because computers lend themselves so well to working with numbers, equations, and calculations, there is useful computer software for the teaching of mathematics, and they will become an increasingly valuable tool for individualizing mathematics instruction.

Since mathematics is the underlying vocabulary of science, the study of biological and physical sciences should be planned at each grade level to utilize the mathematics being taught concurrently. Science should be part of the curriculum from kindergarten through the eighth grade, and three years of science should be required for a high school diploma.

All students, regardless of their interests, are capable of learning basic information in the sciences; scientific illiteracy cannot be tolerated in today's scientifically sophisticated world.

No subjects are more crucial to informed citizenship than those we commonly group under the term *social studies,* yet knowledge of history, economics, government, and physical and economic geography is woefully poor. Social studies must be required throughout elementary and high school. Students must graduate from high school with a solid contextual knowledge of these subjects. Reading lists for older students should include such original texts as Magna Charta, the Federalist Papers, and the Constitution. The *facts* of history and geography—world and American—should be the understructure for vigorous utilization and discussion of current issues and events. Videotapes, public issue television programs, and the daily newspapers are all means toward this end. The classroom is the forum in which students can learn to link what is going on now with knowledge of and lessons from the past.

The teaching of social studies should include frequent student participation in discussions and debates on issues; the subject matter invites such participation and encourages a sense of citizenship as an active and continuing role. Teachers must maintain rigorous standards of accuracy and precision in evaluating written and oral work in these classes, just as they do in English courses. Passion and intensity have a valuable place in the social studies classroom for both teachers and students, but it is important that emotion be rooted in ideas and information, not substitute for them.

As with English, school-board-imposed requirements that check satisfactory achievement are necessary for mandatory social studies courses.

We know from data how uninformed many students are about the political and social world in which they live. We know that vast numbers of Americans do not vote and do not become involved in issues of self-government. We know that rhetoric is often more persuasive than substance, that fewer and fewer people read newspapers, and that more and more get their information from television news broadcasts. We worry that image has become more potent than reality. If this is to change, if we are to develop critical as well as informed intelligence, if we are to shape active, responsible, freedom-loving citizens of tomorrow from the schoolchildren of today, both the content and the way of teaching social studies in our schools must be revitalized.

Every advanced country in the world except the United States teaches its schoolchildren a language or languages other than the native one. This is a standard part of the curriculum because it is recognized that in an interdependent world, communication, competitiveness in world trade, and economic health depend on broad knowledge of other nations, and languages are the access to that knowledge. The teaching of foreign languages must become mandatory in our schools. There have been promising steps toward this already; for example, the Southern Governors Council on International Education has recommended that foreign languages be taught in all schools from the first grade through high school; and the state of Virginia, led by Governor Baliles requires satisfactory foreign language proficiency for graduation. It has established summer language academies to reinforce this program. This and other efforts are steps in the right direction, but we still have a long way to go.

Spelling out curriculum areas that must be required in all schools does not mean that the arts and humanities should be bypassed. Indeed, they can often be integrated with English, mathematics, science, and social studies. When students recognize that the literature and music and art masterpieces that have endured for centuries were created in historical contexts, they will understand both the art and the history better. Competence in science, mathematics, or language is often the foundation for high achievement in other fields; great scientists have often been memorable philosophers and artists.

Throughout the country there are special high schools, from those that concentrate on the arts, physical sciences, or engineering to vocational schools that train students in specific job-related skills. Some specialized schools (sometimes designated as ''magnet schools'') have been created to attract students from a variety of neighborhoods and to promote desegregation without busing to achieve racial balance. Regardless of what their focus or admissions process may be, all special-purpose high schools must teach English, math, science, social studies, and foreign languages as required in general high schools, though obviously there will be subject areas that can be adapted to a school's particular emphasis. Nothing can be allowed to interfere with the basic mission of every school in the country—mastery of subject matter essential for people to live competently and independently, be productive, and *continue to learn throughout life*.

How well this is done should be measured objectively and reported to the public in the spirit of openness, candor, and school-by-school evaluation. As noted below, it is the responsibility of school boards to see that this is done.

Educating the Disadvantaged

With rare exceptions—those few children incapable of learning—all students, regardless of race, ethnic background, economic circumstances, or handicapping condition, must complete the curriculum outlined above. But to require a course of study will not solve the problems of dropouts, illiteracy, or education that is too often education in name only. We need only look at the statistics of failure to know that for many children, equal opportunity has proved more of an ideal for others than a reality for them.

If we are to make education priority number one, we must address this 30 to 40 percent of students who drop out of high school and the issue of how we are going to change lives of dependence and despair to lives of autonomy and promise.

Most of these youngsters are poor and minority. Fortunately we have had twenty years of experience with three education programs that were developed to cope with these problems: Head Start for preschoolers, Title I of the Elementary and Secondary School Education Act (since a recent reenactment, now identified as Chapter I), and the Job Corps. These programs have been in effect since 1965, have only been partially funded, and have in some instances been mismanaged. But out of these years of trial and error, we now know what works and what doesn't.

Head Start was initiated to give potentially at-risk children (those from families living in circumstances that indicate a high probability of school failure and dropout) carefully planned and executed early-childhood learning and reading-readiness experiences before they enter kindergarten and first grade.

Head Start has been remarkably successful over its history. Follow-up studies indicate that it has worked when the children continue to receive the support they need after they enter the regular school program. Indeed, the evidence is so compelling that even David Stockman decided to spare this program from his budgetary ax.

Simply stated, Head Start children do much better academically in elementary and secondary school than low-income and minority children who have not had the benefit of Head Start, and they drop out of school in much lower numbers.

But Head Start has had funding for only a small portion of the children who need it. *There should be a Head Start program available to every low-income and minority child who qualifies.* This should be a top priority for local, state, and federal partnership funding.

At the same time that Head Start was launched, Congress funded a program to provide individualized help, special counseling services, reduced teacher-pupil ratios, and other education services in schools in which there are concentrations of low-income and educationally disadvantaged children. This program, Chapter I, has provided supplemental federal funding to schools in low-income neighborhoods for this extra help. Despite the fact that over $4 billion are currently funded each year, less than half the eligible children in the country have been served.

Each local school district designs and implements its own Chapter I program, and they have been uneven in quality. As a result the success rate has been spotty. It has been effective in many schools across the country and disappointing in others. But with over twenty years of experience, Chapter I evaluations have identified what is effective and what is not. We know too much about what works to continue to support programs that don't.

Delegation of program design and implementation to local school districts was done in the names of autonomy and local control. Any large increase in Chapter I funding to extend services to all students entitled to receive them must be accompanied by strict mandates that only the most successful programs be replicated.

Because funding has never been sufficient, Chapter I has concentrated on kindergarten through grade six, and very few eligible intermediate and high school students have benefited from it. In those rare instances, the program has been successful.

The Chapter I program should be fully funded from kindergarten through high school. This would increase appropriations from the current $4 billion to at least $20 billion a year; and if Head Start is also extended to include all those eligible for its preschool services, I estimate that it would require an additional $7 billion above what we are now spending annually on its very limited program.

At first glance these figures sound formidable. But when we consider the costs of *not* educating these children and youth, of continuing to pour out into our society hordes of ill-educated young people unable to find work or to sustain themselves, the Chapter I and Head Start moneys are the best investment we could make. The funding should be borne at federal, state, and local levels; and program performance should be carefully and regularly monitored. Results are the only criteria on which performance should be judged.

The third program begun in 1965, the Job Corps, provides residential vocational training and academic skills schools for young people who need to be placed in a new environment after years of failure living at home. Students are under care and supervision twenty-four hours a day in their new setting.

Given the hopelessness and despair of the lives they have lived before, it might be expected that these youth, who are extremely difficult to teach, would fare no better in a Job Corps center; but the program has been remarkably successful in training them and placing them in jobs after graduation.

Despite the best efforts of standard school programs, Head Start, and Chapter I, we will always have some young people whose lives have been torn asunder under dreadful environmental circumstances and who are left in the deepest discouragement. They will need the benefits of health care, good nutrition, supportive counseling, and teaching in a wholly new environment. The Job Corps centers have proved they can do the job, and we need four times as many as we now have. A current budget of $600 million should be increased to $2.4 billion.

Like Head Start and Chapter I, funding for the Job Corps should be shared by federal, state, and local governments. New federal legislation to expand these programs should specify this. Programs whose resources are all provided from federal sources attract less local interest and political concern for accountability. Feelings of responsibility and pride are much likelier to be generated when effort and sacrifice are required.

Obviously a fully funded and more rigorously accountable Head Start, Chapter I, and Job Corps will not solve all the problems of educating the more than one-third of our students who fail and quit the education system or others who technically complete school but are not equipped to function independently. But I am convinced that the outcome would be spectacularly different if these three programs became the centerpiece of a nationwide effort to reverse this appalling problem. They merit our support because results show they can work.

They *will* work if we unswervingly apply the wisdom garnered from twenty years of trial and error. They will fail if we are lax, and do not ruthlessly cut those that have yielded mediocre results. This means that the empowering legislation must be tough and unequivocal, and school boards must be responsive and accountable. It also means that we must fund the three programs fully, and not follow past practices of enacting legislation with lofty goals but insufficient funding to carry them out.

Where do we find the $16 billion additional dollars for Chapter I, $7 billion more for a massive Head Start program, and $1.8 billion more for the Job Corps? The federal deficits cry out for budget cuts, not increases. State and local budgets are burdened with the need for more and more services. All this is true; but society is paying far more than this $25 billion in welfare, prison costs, unemployment coverage, and lost revenues from the millions who consume rather than produce taxes. I contend that if these programs are held to strict standards of performance, this additional money will prove to be the best investment we can make.

Federal programs are by no means the only means we should use to deal with the dropout problem. Local school boards, communities, and neighborhoods must initiate stay-in-school campaigns. High schools must replicate dropout prevention plans that have been successful in a few schools, which recruit parental support and foster closer ties between school and home. Remarkable success is occasionally found in schools in the midst of some of our urban ghettos. They have defied the odds, and their students stay in school and achieve. There is much to learn from these unusually effective schools—what they do and how they do it—that has application to other schools across the nation.

What Our School Boards Must Do

School boards have traditionally focused their attention on business affairs and left academic matters to administrators. This must change. They must be much more aggressive, taking concrete steps to govern the schools as assertive policymakers who direct the supervisory and management work of the administrators. They must take full responsibility for implementing state and federal laws pertaining to education. They must set the standards and expectations for academic excellence in the schools they oversee.

School boards appoint superintendents and principals; they also evaluate their performance and set their compensation. The boards have an obligation to foster in their administrators the leadership qualities that are essential to successful schools. Dynamic school boards recognize that their schools can be no better than those they choose to administer them; they therefore devote much time and talent to providing the schools with effective leaders. They know that administrators who implement changes in their schools are subject to many pressures to modify those changes or initiate others. These administrators merit the full support of their governing boards as they do their jobs. Equally, those who fail to perform their leadership duties should be replaced promptly.

To extend the precedent of state-by-state disclosure of educational performance data that began with the release of ED's wall charts, local school boards should maintain a policy of openness and candor about the achievement levels, attendance patterns, and dropout rates of the schools under their governance. A performance profile of each school should be published that includes data on income levels and the number of minority, disadvantaged and handicapped students, as well as academic accomplishments. To make this full-disclosure procedure possible, the school board's policy should require that each student in the school system take a comprehensive examination at a specified time.

School boards must have effective policies that recognize and reward outstanding student and teacher achievement. Achievement is measured by progress and growth as well as by test scores, and policies that recognize this tend to honor students according to their efforts, not simply on the basis of the intelligence with which they are endowed. The boards should develop recognition practices that reach out to their students regardless of background or economic circumstances. Through wise and compassionate policies, the effective school board will provide opportunities for handicapped and disadvantaged students to find their place in the sun too.

For many years the nation's teachers have provided taxpayers with far more education for their children than they have been paying for. School board policies must seek to honor them for their accomplishments and for what they have foregone financially in order to teach. This will obviously not correct the dreadfully inadequate salaries we pay them, but by making a practice of featuring special achievements, the board will provide another way for the community to express its gratitude.

Finally, school boards, administrators, and teachers must persuade the public that education is a community effort not confined to the school. Certainly the policy of candor in reporting school-by-school results will stimulate interest as well as provide information each neighborhood can use in discussing steps needed to upgrade education performance. All parents care passionately about their children's futures and want the best for them. The board's openness will be an eloquent message that education is a community, neighborhood, and family affair and that home, like school, is a place for learning.

Role of Administrators

School districts and schools are growing increasingly more bureaucratic. This is not a new process, but at a time when every possible dollar must be focused on teaching and learning and the activities that support them, it is urgent to fight the growth of nonteaching personnel. A look at the Department of Education's wall charts for 1986 shows that the average total staff-student ratio (all employees, including teachers) was 9.6. The pupil-teacher ratio was 17.9. These figures indicate the proportion of employees in nonteaching capacities. In 1982 the national average ratio for total staff to students was 10.0, so it is clear that the trend to more staff is growing.

Movement conservatives used to tell me that the public schools' organizational structure was fundamentally flawed; they were simply government-operated monopolies free from the discipline and stimulation of marketplace competition. As such, they complained, school administrators and faculty had no incentive to work hard or seek creative solutions to the problems of students and their parents. Some even wanted a constitutional amendment that would mandate a separation between school and state, like the requirement that church and state be separated. They saw no place for government in education on any level—local, state, or national. Education could and should be provided by the private sector.

Extreme, indeed absurd, as these proposals may seem, they do remind us that to the extent that it is possible and advantageous, we should allow more local school autonomy. They also alert us to recognition that the system of public schools as we know it today will not endure if administrators and school boards fail to respond effectively to the demand for reform.

School superintendents must constantly fight growth in nonteaching personnel by keeping the central office lean and limiting support personnel throughout the system to only those employees who are essential to the missions of teaching and learning.

Principals' views of their role must change from that of a branch manager who takes orders from headquarters to that of the head of an individual operation—a school—that is distinctive in itself and thus requires a creative and semiautonomous leader. Principals must be goal directed, performance oriented, and obsessed with a vision of where his or her school is going. Superintendents and school boards must press for this quality and style of leadership in their principals.

The principal's leadership style should set the tone of the school and expand that tone to the neighborhoods and homes in which the students live. Principals must view their schools in a total context that inevitably includes these neighborhoods and homes. To that end, principals must spend more time encouraging, informing, and activating parents to become involved in their children's education so that the home becomes more influential. Children must come to school emotionally and physically fit to learn, and the home as well as the school must motivate and teach.

Obviously no school can fully compensate for failure in the home. Nonetheless, principals must view their role as extending out to where their students spend most of their time. They must strive to reach as many parents as possible, and they must lead their teachers, counselors, social workers, and other support personnel in doing this too.

This responsibility applies most urgently to the homes of children who are likeliest to drop out. The first signs of trouble—poor attendance, excessive tardiness, deterioration in school work, and emotional stress—should be a signal to the school that the student needs help at home.

To reach a nationwide goal of raising the high school completion rate to 95 percent, school administrators must put a strenuous effort into early detection of students at risk of failing or quitting school. Both the central office and the school board must encourage and support principals, teachers, and others who pursue this effort, and each school should put the process of reaching out and enlisting home support high on its weekly agenda.

Principals know that on occasion a few of their teachers may actually work against the process of preventing dropouts; understandably, they greet the departure of some hard-to-educate students with a feeling of relief. Realizing that one disruptive student in a class may be a huge headache, principals should be aware of this and try to solve the problem effectively by vigorously involving the parents.

The central school administrations must provide more special schools and alternative classrooms for students whose behavior interferes with the learning opportunities of others, and they must enlist the efforts of special service personnel in handling the problem. This is obviously an added expense, but it is one that must be borne if we are to succeed in cutting our appallingly high student dropout rate. Greatly expanded Head Start, Chapter I, and Job Corps programs will make more resources and alternatives available for students in need of special help and those whose behavior disrupts classroom learning.

Building a Truly Great Teaching Profession

In 1982 the average teacher salary was $19,274. By 1987 this figure had risen to $26,000. In California and New York these average salaries were $29,132 and $30,678 respectively. There has clearly been some progress in raising teachers' salaries, but they remain appallingly low in many states; South Dakota and Mississippi are examples. In New England, where education has traditionally been held in high public esteem, it is surprising to find the states of Maine, New Hampshire, and Vermont with salaries that are now below those of all the Southern states except Mississippi and Arkansas. Further, it must be remembered that the figures cited above are average salaries; entry-level compensation is much lower.

Over thirty state legislatures have enacted laws to implement career ladder programs that will give teachers opportunities to qualify for promotions without having to move into administration. This has been encouraging, and if sustained it will gradually make the profession more competitive. But we have already begun to see cutbacks in incremental increases that had been scheduled in some career ladder programs, and this is causing bitterness and a feeling of betrayal among teachers and their union leaders who supported the legislation. It is crucial to keep these commitments because the future of the teaching profession depends on maintaining the integrity of the law's intent.

To compete for the best talent on the nation's campuses, where bright students too often choose professions other than teaching, we must have higher entry-level salaries, greater potential for advancement on career ladder programs, a more rigorous teacher-education curriculum, and greater esteem for the profession. Until we can compete in this human talent marketplace, we will continue to have the same problems in the future that we have suffered from in the past.

As with other recommendations for change, the solutions to these problems will be costly. But the nation must face up to the plain and simple fact that we have been getting what we have been paying for. We can't pay low entry-level salaries and offer limited opportunities for promotion and expect a transformation in the quality of new teachers or our ability to hold on to the best. We know from studies of those who enter teaching and then drop out that our top graduates leave within five years, while those lower in their class standings stay on. Not only do we fail to attract our fair share of the most talented into teaching, we soon lose those few who do join us.

This is what I believe must be done to upgrade and then to transform the teaching profession in America:

1. Make career ladder programs standard in all states. Those states that already have them must keep their commitments, and those that have not yet done so should enact the necessary legislation. Every time more money is appropriated for schools, additional funds must be allotted to this long-overdue program.

2. Make entry-level salaries competitive with other professions requiring a similar level of training.

3. Extend teacher education programs to five years. Four years will be spent gaining the baccalaureate degree required for entry into an internship year. This required fifth year would be a combination study and practice experience. It can be taken di-

rectly after college graduation or later, but it must be completed before the new teacher completes a mandatory three-to-five-year probationary period.

4. The teacher education curriculum should emphasize the liberal arts and the subject matter the prospective teacher plans to teach. No majors in education should be permitted at the undergraduate level; they are, of course, appropriate for graduate degrees. Prospective teachers should be admitted to teacher education programs only after careful screening to determine that candidates have an adequate general background in English, mathematics, science, social studies, and the arts and humanities. Admissions officers must be satisfied that the candidate is academically capable and satisfactorily educated.

5. Graduate-level teacher education programs at the nation's top institutions should prepare students to become master teachers. Master teachers are needed as mentors for entry level teachers, and to develop curriculum and instructional materials. Accreditation procedures for these advanced teacher education programs should be rigorous. Graduates should be placed in career ladder programs and in responsible positions in schools.

6. Carnegie studies have recommended establishing national board certification procedures for teachers; this should be pursued as an experimental program designed to upgrade professional preparation and practice in teaching. The concept is worth responsible investigation.

7. Initiatives must be undertaken to attract more minorities into the teaching profession. Minority college students are in comparatively short supply and teaching has been a weak competitor for their skills after graduation. Any school reform plan must provide incentives in the college student grant, loan, and work-study programs that offer special concessions to promising teachers. The federal government should fund this effort as part of its student aid budget.

8. Like law school graduates who must pass the bar examination before being admitted to practice, and accounting graduates who must pass an examination before becoming CPAs, graduates entering teaching should pass an examination before becoming certified to teach. This is now a requirement in thirty-two states and should be put in place in the remaining eighteen.

9. A probationary period for all new teachers, followed by a performance review by a board comprising administrators and senior teachers, should be established as standard practice throughout

the country. The presence of experienced teachers on the panel should provide valuable input and also give them a sense of participation and control over the standards of the profession to which they have devoted their lives. Experienced teachers should also be required to pass reasonable recertification requirements and performance reviews at least every five years. Such programs are in effect in other professions and help assure the maintenance of standards and state-of-the-art knowledge.

10. A board comprising administrators and senior teachers should verify the quality of performance as a requirement for advancement on the career ladder. This will be part of an overall program to recognize and reward demonstrated excellence in teaching as well as seniority. Panel members should be trained to fulfill this role satisfactorily. The participation of teachers as well as administrators will tend to decrease bias and political considerations in the promotion process.

11. To make teachers, and society as a whole, aware of the importance of the profession to the well-being and future of the nation, the status of teaching must be upgraded dramatically. School boards, civic groups, the press, and others must participate in this effort. Teacher recognition and appreciation events should be made a coordinated tradition in communities across the country—a valuable way in which to take public note of their contributions. Obviously, status and respect are established in many other ways as well, not least of which is appropriate pay for an enormously demanding and responsible job that involves the welfare and the futures of our children. But any actions that move us to stop taking teachers for granted should be supported, in the ongoing process of restoring to them the esteem that they deserve.

12. Vigorous teacher recruitment efforts must be made on college campuses and in our communities for several years. There is an urgent need for new talent of high quality to be trained to enter the profession. The recruitment program should have the advocacy and stewardship of college presidents, governors, and the next president.

Financing the Education Renaissance

There is no magical, painless way to fund our schools more adequately. It will cost a lot of money to educate our children in the way I have advocated in these pages, and the only source of these dollars is the taxpayer. If we are to have a satisfactorily educated, productive society, we are all going to have to pay higher taxes.

We should not increase spending without taking the action necessary to see that we get more education for every added dollar. Indeed, we must make current funding levels more productive by searching every budget category for more efficiency and better results. Can we reduce administrative expenses? Can costs of student vandalism be reduced? Should purchasing be centralized or pooled to purchase supplies more cheaply? School systems are large and by their nature bureaucratic, and it is valuable to cast a scrutinizing eye over all bureaucracies at regular intervals to eliminate redundancies and waste and to improve productivity. We must not fail to set priorities for our spending and transfer money from lower to higher priorities in the effort to control costs.

But if we are to bring about a total reform of American education, there is no question about it: It will cost a lot of money.

The federal government should finance at least half the additional cost of fully funding Head Start, Chapter I, and an expanded Job Corps. The funds to pay competitive teachers' salaries, to finance career ladder programs, and to pay the costs of the curriculum, testing, and instructional materials that are needed must also come from a combination of increased taxes and redeployment of other budgetary funds. There will need to be higher education budgets for student aid, for larger enrollments of upward bound low income and minority students, and for teacher education and research.

A major obstacle to school funding in this country has been an overreliance on property taxes. Older Americans who have no children in school and increasing numbers of single adults and childless couples often make local-option tax levies difficult to pass. Most taxpayers meet their tax bills from income, and real property is not a very good measure of the ability to pay taxes. Farmers and others with capital-intensive businesses bear an unfair burden. The tax base determined by assessed valuation of property is often located in property-rich school systems with comparatively few students and low birthrates. We must do more to equalize school revenues by raising funds on the state level and distributing them according to educational need at the local level. This is a task for state legislatures, and some states have made rapid strides in this direction.

Federal support of education is as old as our constitution: the Northwest Ordinance of 1787 included congressional action to fund education—schools and colleges—with revenues from federal lands. We financed vocational education with the Smith-Hughes Act of 1917, and the most successful college student aid program in our history was the GI Bill after World War II. The nationwide benefit accruing from more effective schools makes a good case for more help from Congress. Better education means more productive graduates entering the job market and revenues from the taxes they pay. As we educate the children who would otherwise be likely to join the ranks of the unemployed and illiterate whom we have failed in the past, we can anticipate a more civil society than is now not always the case. This means lower welfare costs and prison costs. The benefits are wide ranging, and they are financial as well as societal.

The American system of public and private colleges and universities is world renowned because of its high quality, diversity, and positive influence. No investment of public funds has ever paid more. Access to our institutions of higher learning must be made available to all those who can benefit from pursuit of a college degree. This requires sufficient student financial assistance, which has traditionally been a federal responsibility.

Funding American education adequately and assuring taxpayers a better quality education in the future than has been the case in the past are both problems and obligations for the next president, the nation's governors, and congressional and legislative leaders. They should be resolved with the same firmness of action that was demonstrated in meeting an enormous transportation crisis during the Eisenhower era. Through a congressionally funded highway trust fund, we built a vast interstate highway system that has transformed the nation. We recognized that our system of roads was outmoded and could not meet the transportation, travel and economic needs of an increasingly complex society. Appropriately placed taxes, such as those on vehicle accessories like tires and batteries, have provided a continuing source of trust fund replenishment.

I recommend a similar approach to funding education reform. Congressional and state action should establish an education reform and renewal trust fund comprised of federal funds matched by state revenues. The trust fund should be administered by the states under federal guidelines. We need concrete, results-oriented leadership that respects the autonomy of the states but expresses federal concern and shared fiscal responsibility for education.

There could be no more farsighted national policy than this. There is no national need more urgent than this. We have set out with bold vision and nationwide commitment in the recent past to address crises that affected the well-being and future of our country and its people, and we succeeded brilliantly—the Marshall Plan, the interstate highway system, and the space program that put a man on the moon. If we answer the clarion call for action on the profound crisis in education, we can make the promise of equal educational opportunity for all Americans a reality. If we summon the will and the resources to deliver on this promise, we, our children, our children's children, and our nation will reap benefits beyond all imagining.

Acknowledgments

||||||||||||||||||||||||||||||||||||||||||||||||||||||||||||||||||||||||||||||||||||||||||||||||||||||||||||||||||||||||||||||||||||||||

Much credit for whatever merit this book may have is due my editor, Ann Harris, whose patience and professional insight are manifested in every chapter. I am also indebted to Erwin Glikes, president and publisher of The Free Press at Macmillan, for his advice and encouragement during the months of effort that have gone into these pages.

Index

Cabinet Photo—Blue Room of the White House—1984

(left to right)
Back row: John R. Block, Raymond Donovan, Malcolm Baldrige, Samuel R. Pierce Jr., William Clark, William J. Casey, Edwin Meese III, William Brock.

Middle row: Terrel Bell, Jeane Kirkpatrick, David A. Stockman, William French Smith, Elizabeth Dole, Donald Hodel, Margaret Heckler.

Front row: Donald T. Regan, George Bush, Ronald Reagan, George Shultz, Caspar Weinberger.